The Minister
and the Care of Souls

HARPER'S MINISTERS PAPERBACK LIBRARY

THE
MINISTER
AND THE
CARE OF SOULS

DANIEL DAY WILLIAMS

HARPER & ROW, PUBLISHERS

New York, Hagerstown, San Francisco, London

Grateful acknowledgment is made to The University of Chicago Press for permission to quote from Carl Rogers, *Psycho-Therapy and Personality Change* (Chicago: University of Chicago Press, 1954), copyright 1954 by The University of Chicago Press.

Chapter 1 of this book is a slightly altered version of an article which originally appeared in *The Union Theological Seminary Quarterly Review,* May 1960, Vol. XV, No. 4, and reprinted here by permission.

THE MINISTER AND THE CARE OF SOULS

First Harper & Row paperback edition published in 1977.

ISBN: 0-06-069491-2

Library of Congress catalog card number: 61-12836

77 78 79 80 81 10 9 8 7 6 5 4 3 2 1

CONTENTS

PREFACE

The Faculty of the Union Theological Seminary in Richmond, Virginia, invited me to give the Sprunt Lectures in 1959, and requested that they deal with the theological foundations of pastoral care. This book gives in substance the content of the lectures. They are a theologian's attempt to analyze the issues involved in the pastoral task. I write as theologian and minister, and claim no special competence in the field of pastoral counseling. I have, however, had the privilege of many years' discussion with those working in this field. I gladly record my debt to Arthur Cushman McGiffert, Jr. and Anton Boisen, whose course, "Experience and Theology," in The Chicago Theological Seminary opened up the relation of theology to psychology for me; to Seward Hiltner, Granger Westberg, and my present colleague, Earl Loomis, with each of whom I have taught courses on the relation of psychiatry and theology; and to William Oglesby of Union Seminary, Richmond, not only for his encouragement in the project I was undertaking, but for helpful criticism of the lectures. The positions taken here are of course my own.

A word should be said about two terms. The Latin *cura* can be translated "care" or "cure," but I prefer "care of souls" because we can always care even when we cannot cure. The "minister" is the ordained person, called by the Church to its leadership in that office. I have used the word "pastor" when the special task of caring for the spiritual needs of the congregation and of individuals is in view. But of course the minister is always a pastor, and the pastor a minister. These are functions as well as offices, and in the broader sense every

9

Christian may be minister-pastor to his neighbor. I have tried to keep this also in mind, and in the last chapter to examine the setting of pastoral care in the life of the congregation.

To know the hospitality of Union Seminary, Richmond, the gracious welcome of its faculty and students, and the loyal and responsive hearing which is given to the Sprunt Lectures is to experience the reality of the Christian community and be sustained by it. I am deeply grateful to President and Mrs. James A. Jones, and to all those who made the occasion of working out this book a memorable one. To my wife I am especially indebted for her critical and competent preparation of the manuscript.

DANIEL DAY WILLIAMS

Union Theological Seminary
New York

CHAPTER 1

THERAPY AND SALVATION:
The Dimensions of Human Need

To bring salvation to the human spirit is the goal of all Christian ministry and pastoral care. In this first chapter we consider the relation between the meaning of salvation in the Christian faith and the healing of the ills of body and mind. That there is a relation has always been affirmed in the Christian Church. Salvation is itself a kind of healing. We speak of our Lord Jesus Christ as the Great Physician who in his earthly ministry, and in the continuing ministry of his Church, is concerned for sick bodies and minds. In the twentieth century a new turn in the "care of souls" has given additional sharpness to our need for a clear view of therapy and salvation. Modern psychological understanding has come as a revolutionary force. So pervasive is its influence that in theological education the analysis of pastoral care has been focused increasingly upon problems of psychotherapeutic counseling, and upon new modes of understanding the pastoral task through the insights of group therapy and group dynamics. It is clear that the movement initiated by Freud has become a broad stream affecting every aspect of religious life.

Some see a danger that a sectarian gospel of psychological healing will be substituted for the Christian message of salvation through God's grace. Others fear that technical preoccupation with methods of counseling will destroy the depth of personal relationship if "souls" become "cases." At this critical juncture it is essential that we in the Christian churches re-examine our theological assumptions in pastoral care. We must know what we are about when we try to see mental and physical illness in relation to human sin and to God's action through which we are forgiven and offered a new life in Jesus Christ.

I. CHRISTIAN FAITH AND KNOWLEDGE

It is necessary at the outset to state my presuppositions concerning the relation of Christian faith to empirical knowledge. I shall affirm two main propositions:

First, the Christian faith arises out of the concrete historical experience of the Hebrew community and the first communities of disciples of Jesus, later called Christians. The faith which gave rise to the Christian community was expressed in the story of Jesus told as the disclosure of God's will to save mankind from the threat of a meaningless, sinful existence. Christian theology is a continuing interpretation of this faith in relation to all human thought and experience.

My second presupposition is that the work of interpreting the Christian faith is never finished. Christ is the *Logos,* the integrating meaning of our existence. Every aspect of experience therefore presents a challenge to the Christian to learn more of God and his purpose. It is God who is the absolute truth, not theology. No theologian should regard any hypothesis which may possibly lead to new knowledge in a spirit of condescension. He may have something to learn about Christ from any human experience. He holds every particular truth to be subject to examination in the light of the ultimate truth which is given to us—but not possessed by us—in Jesus Christ.

In seeking the integrity of the Christian witness as it bears upon the significance of the pastor's task, we recognize that we need all possible scientific and humanistic understanding of human beings and the way they live with one another. We also know that we need the core of personal knowledge which comes only through response to the redemptive love offered in Jesus. The key to pastoral care lies in the Christological center of our faith, for we understand Christ as bringing the disclosure of our full humanity in its destiny under God.

If we find that some psychological perspectives upon human nature lack a full awareness of Christian values—and we certainly shall—we should also remember that in the Church we have had to learn some painful lessons about the inadequacies of much well-intentioned pastoral work. Every human relationship embodies a mystery, and our Christian ministry participates in the deepest mystery of all, the life of the soul before God. We need both the light of faith and the patiently acquired light of empirical understanding if we are to serve God as ministers of his Church.

II. Salvation and Healing

As we set out to analyze the Christian conception of the care of souls, we must say what we mean by salvation. It can be defined as fulfillment for man in a new relationship to God and his neighbor in which the threats of death, of meaninglessness, of unrelieved guilt, are overcome. To be saved is to know that one's life belongs with God and has a fulfillment in him for eternity. This is life eternal, says the Fourth Gospel, to "know the one true God." And the Westminster Confession is echoing this message of the Gospel when it says that "the chief end of man is to glorify God and to enjoy him forever."

The concept of salvation raises many questions. Must every ill of man's flesh or mind be overcome before we can say he is truly saved? When is a person genuinely healthy and fulfilling his intended being? Does the ultimate fulfillment promised in the Gospel lie in a different dimension from the immediate goals of psychological adjustment? If these are related, how are they related? How far does a theological understanding of man tell us anything about the sources of neurotic anxiety and the self-frustration which besets our human life? Is the saved man able to solve more of his problems from day to day, or does he rather learn to live with insoluble problems?

The Scripture appears to take a double attitude toward the healing of disease. God is concerned with the health of man, and the divine power brings healing. At the same time, the biblical man of faith looks beyond present suffering, and assumes a certain indifference toward the immediate ills of life as he anticipates a final fulfillment. It is in the relationship between these two aspects of biblical faith that a theology of salvation and healing must move.

In Old Testament religion, disease and sickness come from the hand of God, as do all the fortunes and circumstances of life (Deut. 29:22; II Chron. 21:18-19). But God is also the healer of diseases. This theme occurs frequently in the Psalms and was the basis of one temple cult. In Psalm 103 the healing of diseases is spoken of in the same breath with God's forgiveness of the sinner, and disease here, as elsewhere in the Old Testament, is to be taken in the literal and physical sense. The same language of healing also appears in the expression of faith in salvation. In Hosea 7:1 God's will to restore his people is declared as his will to heal them. We need a full study of the place of disease and its healing in the Hebrew faith.[1]

The work of healing occupies a large place in the record of Jesus' ministry. However he interpreted healing, as a sign of the Kingdom or as service to men whose heavenly father knows their earthly needs, it must be acknowledged as an essential element in the meaning of his ministry.

In the New Testament faith, as in the Old, the language of salvation and the language of healing are interwoven. H. Wheeler Robinson has pointed out in the analysis of the meaning of salvation *(sōteria, sōzō)* that in the New Testament in one hundred and fifty-one occurences of the noun or the verb, sixteen refer to deliverance from disease or demon possession and over forty to deliverance from physical death.[2] To be made whole is to enjoy the restoration of vital health or function. It is said of the withered hand in Matthew 12:13, "It was restored whole [*apokatastethe*] like the other." Jesus says to the woman healed (Mark 5:34), "Daughter, your faith has made you well [*sesoken*], go in peace and be made whole [*hygies*]"; and Luke reports the ironic rebuke to the Pharisees, "Those who are well [*hygiainontes*] have no need of a physician" (Luke 5:31).

The concern for healing springs naturally from concern for the neighbor. The Christian faith has always recognized the obligation to "feed the hungry and clothe the naked," to visit those sick and in prison. But it is the subtle connection between the natural health of man and the soul's need for salvation which leads to the deeper concerns in the Christian understanding of salvation. The healing miracles in the New Testament appear often as signs of the Kingdom of God. Jesus' power to heal manifests the divine power which restores all of life. Thus the natural desire to be relieved of mortal suffering is transmuted into the question about the meaning of life, and the search for a right relationship to God. It is because of this complex and mysterious relationship between part and whole, natural need and ultimate fulfillment, that Christian theology requires a clear view of the nature of man, and his creature-needs in relation to his destiny under God.

III. In Search of Essential Humanity

A Christian theology of salvation requires a doctrine of essential humanity. From the story of creation to the appearance of the new being in Jesus Christ, the Bible has in view God's intention for his creation and especially his purpose for man, his creature who bears the divine image. Man is intended for fullness of life upon the terms set by his nature as it comes from the hands of God. But the actual state of man is one of estrangement from God, which means a distortion of his essential being. He has not only lost the full life for which he is created, but he has lost in part his capacity to achieve a clear view of what that life is. In our doctrine of man, therefore, we have to respect two elements. First, since man is finite there are limitations to his knowledge of himself and his world which are given with his creaturely state. Man is in process, both in his individual and his collective life. He literally does not know what he is becoming. Even a perfect creature would have to define essential existence in terms which allowed for the limits of creaturely knowledge.

Second, man the sinner has a distorted understanding of his being and of the meaning of his fulfillment. As man searches for his essential self, he corrupts his definition of his humanity. Consider the ideals of humanity which have governed civilizations and see how they are full of the pride of race and class, the selfishness of individuals, and the resentments of finitude and death. Man's search for wholeness can lead him to destruction. So the question of what the real human needs are becomes a theological problem because our ultimate perspective on the meaning of our existence is involved.

In the Christian faith it might appear that the problem has been solved for us by the revelation of our restored humanity in Jesus Christ. He is the archetype of essential humanity. Here is the foundation of the Christian care of souls. We have a guide and criterion for the goal to be sought in every human relationship. But when we ask what this criterion means in actual life, we encounter two special characteristics of the Christian approach to human nature and its fulfillment which are at once the key to insight and the source of perplexity in the pastoral task.

Love is the center of Christ's disclosure of our humanity. God has shown his love for us in the action which reveals his purpose, and that action is told in the Christian story of Jesus. To love then, in the New Testament sense, means to participate in this action. Our action is a response—in ways appropriate to our situation—to what God has done for us. Thus Paul enjoins the Christian community, "Let this mind be in you, which was also in Christ Jesus . . . who took upon him the form of a servant [*doulos*]" (Phil. 2:5 ff.). And this surely is the foundation of Luther's daring statement that we are to become Christ for one another.

So far then we have the basis of all care of souls. It is an action in love which makes concrete the spirit of ministry we know in Christ. But there is a strangeness about such love. It is spirit, never mere form. To love means to conform our action to the concrete needs of the neighbor. Our human need is involved with our guilt, so God's love is expressed as forgiveness. Our need is for hope in the midst of estrangement, so God has to bear with us in our suffering. To know, therefore, that we are to love our neighbor does not tell us what we are to do, until we discover our neighbor's need and learn what we can do. Love becomes in-

carnate in the acts of persons who seek one another in a
spirit which opens the way to a deeper relationship. Adora-
tion, forgiveness, sacrifice, mutuality, are all themes of love,
but none of these allows arbitrary boundaries to its creative
power. Love comes to know itself only in responding to the
call of the neighbor.

There are indeed special dimensions of love in the varied
relationships of life: brotherly love, sexual love, love of
work and play, love of country, love of adventure. None of
these falls wholly outside the meaning of the *agape* of God
made known in Christ, yet in none of them can there be a
mere imitation of Jesus as pattern. The *imitation of Christ*
is either a creative response in freedom or it is a false and
arbitrary imposition of law upon life. All the loves of human
existence may be affirmed in the spirit of *agape,* yet *agape*
transcends them all. It gathers human energies together in
the service of the saving action of God who wills to redeem
every human life from its self-imposed futility.

A second aspect of the Christian criterion of the soul's
health takes us a further step in the consideration of the
meaning of love in the Gospel. We have said that love con-
forms itself to the need to be met. This means that we encounter our neighbor, as God has encountered us, not in
the innocence of a development toward perfection, but in
the distortion and suffering of estrangement. In Tillich's
way of expressing this fact, Christ reveals our essential humanity under the conditions of estrangement.[3] This means
that the Christian revelation does not give us a picture of
a new life, with all problems solved, all perplexity put
away. We see in Christ the way in which love *bears with*
our human situation, taking its burdens into the new life.
Fulfillment is promised, hope is restored, and a new way
opened, but with no setting aside of the conditions of the
human pilgrimage. The restoration of our essential human-

ity as declared in the New Testament is in a sense *proleptic*. We know what we are intended to be. We know love as spirit breaking through and overcoming the darkness of life, but not banishing it. In his great book on the atonement, J. McLeod Campbell said Christ revealed the love of God by trusting it.[4] The trust was declared in the midst of the pain and sin. The resurrection is a sign of the victory which is beginning, but which is not yet consummated.

Therefore, Christian faith has a double aspect in its understanding of what the soul needs. On one hand, every person should be built up into the Body of Christ, the Church. Each is to become in his own way the new man, as God intended. At the same time the concrete decisions in life are to be made in love and trust, allowing the spirit of love and specific circumstance to open the way.

As one reads the New Testament the wonder grows that in spite of the fact that the first Christians were overwhelmed by the assurance that they had seen in Christ the new Adam, man restored and fulfilled, they refused to make Christ a new law. He is himself the fulfillment of the law.[5] Throughout the Gospel runs the theme that there is yet more to be known of the riches of God's purpose. "Greater things than these will ye do," says the Christ of the Fourth Gospel to his disciples. "It doth not yet appear what ye shall be," says the Johannine writer (I John 3:2). And Paul returns always to this theme: "The earnest expectation of the creature waiteth for the manifestation of the sons of God." "We wait for the redemption of our body, for we are saved by hope" (Rom. 8:19, 23-24).

What then does it mean to be saved? It means to have one's life in all its good and evil, its hope and its brokenness, restored to participation in the love of God, which is the meaning of all existence. This participation is not simply the enjoyment of a legal status; it is a new relationship of personal faith. It is the broken man becoming whole. There is a present and positive renewal in the life of faith. It is not only being rescued from evil, it is the discovery of the wonder of the good world and the glorious goodness of the creation. To be saved is to be led out of self-centered concern to a joyful and active vocation, serving God in his world.

Salvation contains a dimension of expectation. "Beloved, now are we the sons of God, and it doth not yet appear what we shall be" (I John 3:2). Thus the Christian conception of eternal life unites the present experience of God's abiding grace with the expectation of a life with him which neither suffering nor death nor anything else can destroy. It involves a task to be accomplished and a glory to be celebrated. And these belong together.

IV. SUFFERING AND SALVATION

When we recognize that salvation for the Christian has its definition in the story of Jesus and at the same time that the Gospel raises our eyes to an infinite horizon which stretches beyond all our knowledge of what human life may become, we recognize two consequences for the way in which we understand the Christian ministry to people.

The first of these is that there is always more to learn about human needs, and the way they should be met. Such learning involves both the gathering of objective knowledge and the practice of personal ministry. There is much we can know about man only through the patient fact-gathering and experimentation of the sciences. Physiology, biology, psychology, anthropology, sociology, indeed even physics and chemistry, are making continual discoveries which are relevant to our knowledge of man. Man is incredibly complex, and that fact is critically important for the task of pastoral care. This is not to say that we need to have complete scientific knowledge about a person before we can communicate the essential message of salvation. But the spirit of ministry to another human being leads us to respect and use all the knowledge we do have. Even the spirit of *agape,* by itself, will not necessarily protect us from dangerous errors which may lead to the hurt and even the destruction of others. The pastor who seeks to help a paranoid by sympathy alone or by offering only the consolation of prayer and religious assurance is not really feeding the hungry person or giving the cup of cold water. Love requires intelligence in action.

We know, however, that we can add up all the objective knowledge we derive from the sciences and still miss the kind of knowledge which comes only from personal participation with others in man's search for reality. One of the genuine services of psychology to Christian ministry in our day has been the recovery of the insight that this element of personal participation in relationship is vital to our discovery both of the other person and of ourselves. It has also been a contribution of the psychological sciences to show that such knowledge is not contradictory to scientific objectivity. The I-Thou relationship is not an esoteric experience separated from all the other structures of human existence. It is rather the center of a process which has many structural elements, and in which objective knowledge has its very important place. Those who emphasize personal relationship and acceptance often forget the discipline and preparation which have gone into the experience of the counselor or pastor who has developed the habits, insights, and skills which open the way to fruitful personal meeting.

The Christian understanding of salvation, we conclude, requires a continuing dialogue between Christian believers and the sciences of man. It excludes dogmatism on either side. William Ernest Hocking reminds us that most of our conscious life is engaged in trying to find out what we really desire.[6] Even in the new life of faith in which desire is being transformed, we must still ask for the meaning of our new existence in its concrete implications.

The second consequence of the meaning of salvation leads to some basic issues with modern views of man and with some modern psychologies, for it has to do with the attitude which Christian faith takes toward the continuing ills of life, toward the meaning of suffering, and toward the natural goal of the complete health of the well-adjusted person. Christianity, we say at once, is concerned with the life of faith as man's discovery of how to bear with his limitations as well as how to overcome them. St. Augustine goes to the heart of the matter in his vision of the two aspects of the revelation in Christ:

He is at once above, and below; above in Himself, below in His people, above with the Father, below in us. . . . Fear Christ above, recognize him below. Have Christ above bestowing His bounty, recognize Him here in need. Here He is poor, there He is rich. . . . So then Christ is rich and poor. As God He is rich, as Man poor. Yea rich now as Very Man, He hath ascended into heaven, and sitteth at the right hand of the Father; yet is He still poor here, is ahungered and athirst and naked.[7]

Let us illustrate what this view of Christ implies in the crucial question of guilt. There is real guilt, the consequence of a freedom exercised without love or within a self-centered love. There is a pathological "guilt-feeling" in which our sense of remorse is out of all proportion to the regretted action. There are the consequences of guilt, sometimes engraven on our physical being, with disease resulting from the inner tension.

Now the Christian Gospel promises relief from the burden of real guilt. God's forgiveness has been and is offered. It is effective in our midst. To believe in Jesus Christ is to know that God has crossed over to us, when we could never find our way back to him through our own effort. We have been delivered from the body of death.

Shall we describe this deliverance, then, as freedom from any continuing struggle with the isolation of guilt, and from any pathological guilt feeling, as well as from the disease which comes with inner tension? Sometimes the Gospel has been understood in this way; but it ought to be clear that there is something wrong with such a view. We should not forget that the new existence in reconciliation is given in and with the human realities of sin and estrangement. The notion that through faith we cease to be people in need of forgiveness has led to some of the most fanatical and unlovely aspects of Christian history. We may agree that Calvin's language is subject to misunderstanding, but surely he is right when he says of the saints that "though sin ceases to reign, it continues to dwell in them, there remains in them a perpetual cause of contention, to exercise them, and not only to exercise them but also to make them better acquainted with their own infirmity."[8]   *Rom 6/7*

Calvin implies here that continuing struggle is a source of deepening knowledge to the Christian. This suggests one answer to the place of suffering in the growth of the soul. Let us examine two alternative answers which have persisted in Western culture and which reappear in some contemporary psychological interpretations of man. The first is the Stoic way. The self is guarded against threatened destruction through an inner strength which makes itself invulnerable to the assaults of outrageous fortune. The protection is partly a strength to withstand and it is partly a protective shield, for the Stoic will not let himself be moved by suffering more than he can help. What he must feel he will endure.

There is truth in the Stoic answer, and the essential ele-

ment in it is not foreign to the Christian spirit. There is a
necessary stoicism in the practical wisdom of life, even for
those who believe that all suffering may lead to creativity.
But the Christian view is never purely Stoic, for the Christian is not ultimately concerned about protecting himself
from suffering. In the involvements of love we seek to
share life, not immunity to its pain. Identification with the
needs of the neighbor is possible only through a willingness
to become vulnerable. Jesus was a man of sorrows and
acquainted with grief.

The second way of dealing with suffering is the Epicurean
way. Let us create for ourselves, it says, an island of harmony
and satisfaction in the midst of the chaos of life. In order
to distill the creative essence of life we must shun its gross
evils, wall ourselves off from as much of its suffering as we
can, and shape life to yield gratification of all our instincts
and capabilities. It is a mistake to think of the Epicurean
way as a crude affirmation of the search for pleasure. It
requires a discipline in its search for the possibilities of the
good life, and that is, in Epicurean terms, the satisfying life.

Both the Stoic and the Epicurean ways can be found im-
plicit if not explicit in various psychological doctrines. A
strain of the Epicurean search for self-fulfillment runs
through many psychologies whose inspiration goes back to
Freud's first formulation of the pleasure principle. In the
early Freudian doctrine man's vital energy seeks nothing but
its gratification. Everything must be subordinated to its release, for it will shape its own patterns of fulfillment.

But Freud, with his realistic sense, saw that civilization
cannot exist on the basis of the libido's gratification alone.
The very demand for work with its necessities of discipline
makes that impossible. So Freud found a final contradiction
between the nature of man and the necessities of his existence. Civilization must always rest in part on discontent.

Later, Freud thought he had found in the death instinct an apparatus within the self sufficiently powerful to hold it to its work in spite of the pleasure principle. Erik Erikson sees Freud's final doctrine as really a stoicism reaffirmed at the point of the failure of the epicurean principle. *"Das Leben auszuhalten:* to stand life, to hold out," becomes the only way.[9]

It is noteworthy that a later Freudian, Herbert Marcuse, in his *Eros and Civilization,* seeks to rescue the epicurean principle on the basis that modern technology can relieve so much of the burden of painful work that man can begin to think of a completely eroticized and gratifying civilization. Even death itself may somehow be taken into the soul's fulfillment and *eros* and *agape* become one.[10]

We have come here to a crucial issue between the Christian faith and these alternative styles of life. It is true that Christianity has always sought the relief of human suffering. It is concerned with bodily and mental health, and affirms the goodness of human powers and their development in strength. But that which is deepest in Christian faith moves against both stoicism and epicureanism.

The Christian ideal of life envisions something higher than freedom from anguish, or invulnerability to its ravages. Its goal cannot be the perfectly adjusted self. In the world as it is, a caring love cannot but regard such a goal as intolerably self-centered. What does it mean to be completely adjusted and at peace in a world as riddled with injustice, with the cries of the hungry, with the great unsolved questions of human living as this? We see why in the end we cannot identify therapy for specific ills with salvation for the human spirit. To live in love means to accept the risks of life and its threats to "peace of mind." Certainly the Christian ministry to persons is concerned to relieve physical ills, anxieties, inner conflicts. But this relief of private burdens is to set the person free to assume more important and universal ones.

Erich Fromm, the neo-Freudian who has contributed greatly to the analysis of contemporary man's psychological problems, is much less convincing when he seeks to define a philosophy of life. He proposes the conception of the free individual and rejects the Christian conception of man as the servant of God: "to live productively, to develop fully and harmoniously,—that is *to become what we potentially are.*"[11] But Fromm's "productive personality" reflects the end product of an age so confident of techniques that it has forgotten or wants to avoid the ultimate problems of human existence. This harmonious personality enjoying the satisfactions of the "sane society" is for all his apparent psychological health still a utopian ghost unfitted even to survive in this world, let alone become genuinely productive in human relationships. The measure of man's life is not his freedom from inner struggle, but his discovery of how the whole of life, including its dark side, can be brought into the service of growth in love.[12] In this sense salvation must transcend all particular therapies.

V. The Principle of "Linkage"

We seem, then, to return to the initial question of the Christian concern for psychological and physical healing, and we have not found a full answer. Why should the ministry of healing seek a deep reconciliation between the search for health and the search for salvation?

I propose that the fundamental theological connection of salvation and therapy is found in the nature of man. There is a principle which needs to be explored in every Christian anthropology, and which is being disclosed in its full significance only with the help of modern psychology. I will call it the principle of "linkage" in human existence. Man,

God's creature, is the being who finds every part of his
experience linked with every other part. This point is sometimes made with the formula that man is a "whole." That
is true, but too simply true. The real situation is that man
is both whole and parts, mind and body, a flow of experiences, and a responsible, searching self. What has to be
recognized is the significance of the fact that every part of
his being and his experience is linked actually or potentially
with every other part. There is no happening in the history
of the body or mind which may not involve the whole person at the spiritual center of his existence. A trivial incident
may open the way for the first time to the discovery of oneself and of God. A light illness may become the occasion
for facing the ultimate issues of life. The struggle with a
neurosis may become the focal point of the wrestle of the
soul with God. We know that this happens. We need to
know much more about why and how it happens.

We begin to see that there are two major modes in which
the parts of experience affect the whole of it. In one context
there are direct causal relationships between one event and
the person's reaction. A glandular deficiency produces an
emotional disturbance. A successful venture produces a
new sense of wonder and gratitude. A recovery from illness
opens the way to reflection on the goodness of God.

In the second mode the relationships between experiences
are mediated by their function as symbols. A struggle to
understand another person becomes a symbol of the mind's
search for understanding life itself or God himself. Loving
devotion to a sick person becomes a sacrament of the spirit
of God who cares for all. This is one reason why we need
to learn much more about the sacramental aspects of the
search for healing. The hunger of the body may become the
symbolic expression of the hunger of the soul for God.

There is much we do not know about the linkage of

experiences with the spiritual growth of man, and about
the mutual reinforcement of what I have called the direct
causal relationships and the symbolic relationships. Certainly they are intimately woven together in all human life.
But once we have grasped the principle of linkage we see
how meaningless a sharp distinction between therapy and
salvation becomes.

To take an illustration from academic life. Every professor now and then must talk with a student who finds it
impossible to get his papers written. Here is a moment of
crisis which can lead to trouble or to deeper self-understanding. One can say that nothing in the student's or the professor's salvation depends on solving this problem. That may
be true, or it may not be true. This may be the occasion
for the facing of issues which go to the roots of a person's
being.

It may be that the problem is a trivial one, unconnected
with any major orientation of the person, or it may be the
signal of a severe mental illness or of a crisis in personal
faith. We cannot know beforehand, and that is precisely
the point. Given the linkage of the parts of our experience
with the whole, there is no way of knowing without living
through the problem with the person just what it means
to him and to his relationship to God. The very process of
working the problem through may create new connections.
And the process of working it through may transform its
meaning.

No one can say a priori how far the solution to particular
problems will include an acceptance of certain limitations
which must be lived with, because they will never in this
life be removed. The real healing of the spirit may come
just at the point where limitations are acknowledged and
are taken into the person with courageous acceptance.

From a Christian point of view, then, human needs must

be met on two levels. There is the obvious insistent need of the body and the mind for that which sustains and nourishes. But the immediate problem may be the door through which we walk into the arena where ultimate questions are asked and answered. The search for therapy is transmuted into the quest for salvation. Luther's statement can stand as a paradigm for Christian experience: "I did not learn my theology all at once, but I had to search deeper for it, where my temptations took me."[13]

What were Luther's temptations? We know something about them, but not all. No one can ever know fully the experience of another. What we do know is that each of us must come to his meeting with God bearing his private burden in his own way. Those who came to Jesus found both the message of the Kingdom and healing for specific ills. The concern for therapy and the message of salvation lead us into a strangely and wonderfully ordered human existence. Psychologists and ministers face to face with the person can learn from each other and both will be humbled by the mystery before which they stand.

CHAPTER 2

THE MINISTER'S AUTHORITY

In the first chapter we saw how salvation and healing are linked in human living. Now we must consider the relationship of the Christian pastor to the person with whom he counsels on matters of the soul's sickness and health. Pastoral care extends far beyond the personal counseling of individuals. We shall say more about the significance of the Church as a saving community in the last chapter; but here we concentrate on the pastor's responsibility when a person comes to him for guidance. We meet at once the question of the authority of the minister and of his office. There is no place in the life of the church where the issues concerning the nature of the minister's authority become more sharply defined or where they lead to more fateful consequences than at the point where he becomes responsible for a soul in need. We know that the way in which we conceive our ministry is of critical importance in determining whether there will be healing or failure. Wrong conceptions, distortions, repressed resentment of authority, can get in their destructive work where pastor and person meet. We have to ask how a right theology of authority enters into the practical task of pastoral care.

The significance of the claim for the authority of the Christian minister has been vividly depicted in a motion

picture made in France. It tells of a Roman Catholic community on an offshore island in which the people have
behaved so badly that the bishop withdraws the priest from
the parish, and for a time deprives the entire community
of the Mass.

As the people try to adjust to this new situation, a man
of strong character who has been serving as caretaker of the
church asserts his leadership. He calls the people together
in the church, and tremblingly mounts the pulpit to tell
them that they must gather on Sundays for prayers and
hymns, and strive to make their peace with God. As the
story unfolds, a young woman in the community becomes
desperately ill and has to be taken to the mainland in an
effort to save her life. This lay "pastor" takes her in a
small boat across the rough sea. The woman believes she is
dying and asks him to hear her confession and give absolution. The climax comes in the agony of his decision as to
whether he can presume to do this. What right has he,
without ordination, to hear a soul's confession and to speak
the divine word of forgiveness?

Some who stand in a Protestant tradition may be inclined
to regard such hesitation at assuming priestly authority as
a Roman Catholic peculiarity. But on a deeper view no
Christian minister or layman escapes the profound mystery
of confession and absolution. How is it possible for us men
to speak of God's word to another? The recurrence of the
theme of "unofficial priesthood" in much contemporary
literature, such as the novels of Silone, suggests that the
question of the spirit and authority of the ministry is close
to the surface in all Christian cultures in our century.

I. Authority and Ministry

We get important light on our problem when we see that
in the New Testament authority and ministry are insepar-

able. God's word in Jesus Christ is his expression of divine authority in history. Christ is the Way, the Truth, and the Life. The disclosure of ultimate authority comes through Christ's ministry. He takes upon himself the form of a slave, and becomes obedient to death, wherefore, Paul says, God has exalted him (Phil. 2:5-10). We rightly use "servant" instead of slave for the New Testament *doulos* because Jesus freely gives his life. He is not an automaton. Divine authority and power are made known through a life of service voluntarily chosen and lived in uttermost love. "The Son of man came not to be ministered unto, but to minister" (Matt. 20:28). Authority always means the exercise of power in accord with some source of legitimacy. There is an authentic order which connects the valid claim to authority with reality. In the New Testament Jesus' power and right to express divine truth among men are inseparable from his ministry. It is *as the Servant* that he bears supreme authority.

If we hold, as I believe we must, that authority in the Christian Church is finally personal and spiritual, the reason lies here in the mode of God's self-revelation. We learn who God is, in the fullest way open to us as men, through his self-expression in the man Jesus.

Thus all ministry in the Church takes its meaning from Christ's ministry. We can agree with T. W. Manson:

. . . we see a ministry whose norm is the ministry of Jesus—servant of all; servile to none—and a liberty of the Spirit that does not degenerate into license.

This means that we take the organic conception of the Church in deadly earnest. When we do that, we find only one essential and constitutive Ministry, that of the Head, our Lord Jesus Christ. All others are dependent, derivative, functional.[1]

If we hold such a view of the personal nature of authority, we are free to recognize the development of many forms of the ministerial office as an inevitable and valid aspect of the history of the church. There is no need to recall here the story of that development, though we should not forget that the history of pastoral care has been bound up with various conceptions of ecclesiastical office and power. John McNeill's *A History of the Cure of Souls* and the essays in *The Ministry in Historical Perspectives* treat the history in significant detail.[2]

In our concern for pastoral care, we may hold different views of the historical development of the pastoral office and the ages-long debate as to the proper form of the ministry. We know there has been tension throughout between charismatic and institutional doctrines of the legitimate ministry in the church. And however we may emphasize the spiritual and personal aspects of ministry, we cannot escape the fact that every outburst of spiritual energy as it broke through old forms at the same time used those forms. When it destroyed old ones, it also shaped new types of formal ministry. The history of such spiritual sects as Quakers and the Disciples of Christ is just as instructive in this matter as that of the Catholic orders. The call to ministry is ultimately dependent on the spirit which bloweth where it listeth, yet it normally requires to be brought into connection with historical forms of the Christian community.

We may say, then, that there is authority in the *office* of Christian ministry, and in the pastoral function of that office. The Christian minister enters into a distinctive relationship to the Church and to the people of a congregation when he is ordained. The precise definition of that new relationship is notoriously difficult. Indeed, some of its aspects will always escape clear analysis, for there is the mystery of the new life in the Body of Christ surrounding it. We must avoid any view which separates pastor from people, for Christ's ministry is there wherever his work is being done. Yet the minister-pastor in the church is primarily responsible for presenting the truth and demands of the Gospel in preaching, in leadership, and in the care of the congregation. No adequate view of the ministry can avoid recognition of this representative character of the ministerial office. There are very different views of how the representative character of the office is established in the Church, and there are different views of the way in which the authority it involves is conferred and can be exercised. But we see in every actual ministry an office and a vocation which involve the special responsibility of the Christian minister for presenting to the church and representing in the church the ministry of Christ which brought the Church into being.

This special character of the ministry as sacred office constitutes a major resource in dealing with the sick soul; but it also gives rise to real problems. Distorted notions of what the ministry is and of what ministers are like as persons can obstruct effective counseling. There are, for example, the attitudes of submission and of resentment which often lurk beneath the surface of an apparently straightforward acceptance of the ministry and what it stands for. What we are here emphasizing is that the pastoral counselor does his work within the structure of the pastoral office. This is true whether or not he explicitly uses Christian language or any special Christian symbols in a particular situation. It is of greatest importance, therefore, to see clearly what the minister's authority means, and what its limits are.

II. The Claim and the Gift

The minister presents a Gospel which has two themes: the claim of God and the gift of God. We need to examine both of these.

To begin with the claim and demand. The minister de-

sires to help people, but he begins with the conviction that
God has set the pattern of life and determined the conditions under which there can be real help. "No man is an
islande" in the great words of John Donne. That means not
only that each life is bound up with every other, but that
man is beholden to his Creator, who has made him and
established the boundaries of his spirit. We do well to under-
line this Christian perspective as we approach the pastoral
task. It constitutes one of the clear and specific differences
between the pastoral relationship and many other counseling
relationships. We are not forgetting the freedom of the
Gospel and its promise of freedom to the human spirit; but
are saying that in the Christian view all freedom has its
conditions set by the creative action of God in determining
the conditions of life. One thinks of John Oman's word,
"Sin is the attempt to get out of life what God has not put
into it."[3]

The claim which God makes is in one of its aspects
ethical. The first obligations of life are love to God and
to the neighbor. We rightly think of pastoral care as an
effort to bind up wounds, to heal the sick, and an encouragement to bear the pain of life. But the Christian knows that
the fulfillment of any life depends upon discovery that life
must be lost for Christ, that it must be given in love to a
center outside oneself. Personal satisfaction does not con-
stitute the goal of life. To live in fellowship with God and
the neighbor is the secret of the soul's fulfillment.

One of the weaknesses of our culture is our desire to be
rid of the ills of body or mind without taking account of
the iron necessities of life and the ultimate law of self-giving.
This is one reason why an emphasis on healing alone can
threaten the morale of the Church. The truly healthy in
spirit do not expect life to offer them a cure for every ill.
There can be no real health of spirit until we come to

terms in humility and repentance with our self-centeredness. We see, then, that the moral dimension of life has its place at the basis of pastoral care. Strength of soul has many roots, and it is true that many of them lie deeper than the acceptance of the moral law; but God has given that law to his creation, and knowledge of that law is, as for the Apostle Paul, one ingredient of the knowledge of God, and therefore of a true self-knowledge.

The claim of God also transcends the moral dimension. "Thou shalt have no other gods before me" is more than a summons to obedience to law. It is the claim of the Creator upon the whole being of his creature. To accept it is to know the true center of life and hope. The Christian counselor knows that there is no final solution of the ills of life other than through faith in God. He will not treat the meaning of that faith as an addendum to his pastoral work. It constitutes the very foundation of the care of souls.

Since our position here raises questions about the "permissive" spirit in counseling, it is interesting to observe the way in which Erich Fromm treats this problem of whether life can be understood without faith in God. Fromm wisely sees that even from his humanist perspective the issue concerning God cannot be set aside. He takes the view that while man cannot know the true God he can discover and identify the false gods, and exclude them from his loyalty.[4] But surely this is a quite unstable position. How can one know a god to be false unless he has some sense of what the true God would be? And such insight must of necessity contain an element of genuine knowledge of God. But Fromm is right in recognizing that questions of ultimate meaning are involved in the search for health of body and mind.

Alongside the claim of God, and inseparable from it, there is his gift. The same Lord who claims all of life for himself and for the community of loving service is the gracious God who "forgives all your iniquity and heals all your diseases," as the Psalmist sings (103:3).

We shall look more deeply in the following chapters at the meaning of forgiveness, but here we need to stress that forgiveness has both a moral and a transmoral aspect. It is God's action in standing by the sinner and reconstituting the relationship broken by our wrongdoing. Sin is not only the breaking of the divine law; it is personal estrangement, it is the separation of man from the true source of his being. It is the life created for love twisted into the life of love-lessness. The gift of God is his powerful invasion of the disordered life we create for ourselves, and his persuasive power to set us in a right relation again.

It is toward the grace of forgiveness that the minister would point all who seek God. When he speaks of forgiveness he is not merely announcing a doctrine which the Church teaches, but he is declaring a present and powerful reality. The very office of minister, which far too often is understood to symbolize only judgment upon sin, should be known as one expression in the Church of the forgiving spirit. We have said that to be a minister is to enter through a public vocation and office into a responsible continuation of the ministry of Christ whose ministry was the disclosure of the gracious will and the forgiveness of God. To minister in Christ's name is to accept the vocation of witnessing in a public way in the Church and the world to the grace which Christ has brought.

Three aspects of this high view of the ministry can be briefly stressed. First, the minister's representation of the claim and the grace of God is not something which belongs to him simply as an individual, but to him as he stands within the community of believers, the Church, which God has brought into being through his gracious action. One protection against some common misunderstandings is to keep clear this fact that the minister has his vocation only in dependence upon the whole community of faithful and needy people. He is one with them. Therefore, the Christian minister has as the keystone of his calling the truth that he stands under the judgment of God and in need of forgiveness. A wise chaplain in an American prison was once asked what he regarded as the prime requirement for an adequate ministry to those in prison. At once he replied, "To realize that you are in the same need of grace as these men who are sent here."

The second point is that the office of ministry creates certain temptations and possibilities of injury to the minister and to others. There is, for example, the fact that he can use the office and its powers as a protective device against facing himself. He can further use the office in various ways to acquire special status or achieve power over other people. This can happen quite unconsciously as well as deliberately. What honest minister will not confess that he has been guilty of such misuse of the sacred office at some time under certain stress?

In the third place, we recognize the inevitable tendency of the ministerial office to separate clergy from laity. This can be true actually even when it is denied theologically. Church history is partly the tragedy of clericalism and anti-clericalism. There is collective guilt as well as individual guilt in this history. The guilt is on both sides, but ministers never should forget that when they encounter the resentment, the misunderstanding, or sometimes just the plain ignorance of what the Christian ministry is, they are in part seeing the consequences of the sins of the Church and churchmen through the centuries. The very fact that the minister deals with sacred symbols, and standards may make it in some cases most difficult to get down to the reality underlying those symbols. Voltaire's jibe that of course God will forgive, since it is his business, really points to a profound problem in the spiritual life. All organizing and routinizing of the great experiences must at some point become a threat to the spirit. That, at least, is a good working assumption to put us on our guard. It is a theme which Nicolas Berdyaev expressed discerningly in his view that history is "the tragedy of spirit."[5] If Berdyaev exaggerated the tension between form and spirit, he still saw the problem in its full dimensions.

A positive meaning can be drawn from these acknowledgments of the pitfalls of the ministry. It is that the minister can be bold to act in the name of God and in the truth of the Gospel just because he belongs within the community which God has created out of his sovereign act of forgiveness. It is by faith alone that any Christian can minister to another person, and any Christian minister can preach or teach or counsel. Faith in Christian language does not mean a sheer leap in the dark. It means personal response to God's action in Christ. It means to stand within the orbit of God's grace and acknowledge one's absolute dependence upon God for a new life of hope and love.

We learn of the divine self-identification with sinners as we see the story of Jesus unfold in the New Testament. We see Jesus maintaining an unbroken devotion and love toward God; but he does not separate himself from the sins of men or the consequences they entail. As Donald Baillie says concerning the Gospel record of Jesus: "He did not set up at all as a man confronting God, but along with sinners who do not take this attitude he threw himself solely on God's grace. The God-man is the only man who claims nothing for himself but all for God."[6] A ministry in the spirit of Christ has no place for pride of status or exemption from judgment. Its authority lies elsewhere.

III. The Person in Need

In our inquiry for the source of ministerial authority we must next give our attention to the person to whom pastoral care is given. Who is this person who comes to the pastor with a burden, a bewilderment, perhaps a flaming hatred? What does it mean that he seeks out a pastor or is thrown into a situation where a pastor may hear his story? The Christian answer to these questions is startling. This person is Christ himself standing before the minister. Christ, the Son of God, is in reality present wherever man is. Christ is not only present in the world through *our* Church and *our* ministry. What a false and wrongheaded notion it is that Christ is present only where we Christians are! Christ is wherever men are living, hoping, suffering. The text here is Jesus' word, "Inasmuch as ye have done it unto one of the least of these my brethren, ye have done it unto me" (Matt. 25:40). This truth affects the pastoral relationship profoundly and we must explore it further.

Christ is present in the person in the obvious sense that the purpose of God, made known in Jesus Christ, is the fulfillment of God's Kingdom in all of life. Christ is therefore present in every person as the ultimate meaning and reality which leads to the fulfillment of God's will for life. This does not mean that the Christian serves others for the sake of obedience to an abstract principle which he names "Christ." It means that in the Christian view Jesus Christ is the person through whom we know concretely the personal reality at the heart of God's purpose for the world. In Christ we see God's will to create a community of persons. That is to say, we know who each person is, in the ultimate significance of his life, as we know him "in Christ."

Paul's phrase "in Christ," which he used more than any other single expression, cannot be fully explicated until we all "know as we are known"; but Paul surely means that in the Christian life we are not only separate individuals, but we are incorporated into the new reality which God has created in history through the life of Jesus. We must keep in view, therefore, the fully personal meaning of being "in Christ." It is not absorption or destruction of personality, but its fulfillment. Christ is "being formed in us" as we enter fully into our humanity through the gracious action of God, who has broken through our old and estranged ways and established the foundations of the new life.

To see every person as created for life "in Christ" is the key to the meaning of Christian "realism" in dealing with persons. Such realism does not mean passing over the reality of sin, the evil in the human heart, or the inexplicable tragedy of the suffering in creation. It is in the midst of these realities that the story of Jesus has its meaning. But realism means knowing that each person has been created in God's image and is capable of being open to the grace of God and of beginning to love. We cannot say that pastoral care depends on the assumption that we, or—to put it bluntly—even God, will find a way to solve every problem man faces. We can speak only of the way in which Christians understand the hope which guides our dealing with the ills of the soul and body of man. We must take a clear view of the medical realities of disease and the spiritual realities of sin, but it makes a difference in the pastor's understanding of all human ills that he sees every person as created for a life of love to God and his neighbor. We can understand many ills of the spirit and even of the body as caused by the damming up of the way to a life of free and self-giving love. We will not leave out of account in meeting any problem the possibility of uncovering resources in the human spirit of courage and power to love.

We can take a further step in learning the significance of

the presence of Christ in the person. We have been speaking
from the point of view of the pastor's concern for the person
in his need. But to recognize Christ in the person is to see
that he is a bearer of grace to the pastor. Christ is present
as the One through whom we ever receive more than we give.
Sometimes we receive grace through discovering the understanding, courage, and capacity for forgiveness in the other
person who is struggling for light and peace. There is no
minister who knows what he is about who has not been renewed again and again through discovering in others, even
those in desperate need of help, a strength upon which he
himself drew afresh.

The grace of Christ can be released through the new
relationship into which a pastor and his people enter. There
are times when it is given to him to enter with another into
the deepest level of searching for insight, for healing truth,
and sharing the joy of discovery. Such experience is the product of no technique by itself. It is the gift of God to those
who are open to the full adventure of searching for truth.
We have already recalled Martin Luther's declaration that
we are to become Christ for one another. We do not take the
place of Christ, but we enter into a relationship where he
is present through what we give of him to one another in our
broken ways.

There are many implications of this conception of mutual
dependence in the pastoral relationship. We cannot reduce
them to formulas; but the clear conclusion from this way of
seeing the pastoral task is the recognition that one of the
surest aids to an effective pastoral care is to think of the pastor
as involved in the needs, the suffering, the adventure of the
spirit to which he brings the insight and concern of his office.
He is a participant in the story of sin and sickness and restoration. It takes place again through and in him as he becomes a
pastor to others.

IV. The Nature of Pastoral Authority

We have been searching for the nature of pastoral authority and we have been led to an analysis of the pastoral relationship itself. That relationship has some radical implications for the meaning of authority in the Church.

In the New Testament, as we have seen, the authority of Christ and his ministry are bound together. Pastoral care is service to persons in the spirit of Christ. The principle we now have to grasp is that the authority of the pastor is not something merely brought into the pastoral relationship, but is born out of that relationship. I am taking the view that the authority of the Christian minister, that is, his authority to speak and act as a representative of the Gospel of God's forgiveness and his healing power, is given only through the actual exercise of the pastoral office. Real personal authority arises out of the concrete incarnation of the spirit of loving service which by God's help becomes present in the care of souls. And this means that ministerial authority can be lost as well as won.

In taking this position I do of course raise a very old question in the doctrine of the ministry, the question of whether the minister's authority to preach the Word, administer sacraments, and act as pastor inheres in his office and ordination or whether it inheres in his person and is dependent upon his faith. But need we make a simple choice between these? Surely authority inheres in the office of ministry, for that office is the Church's expression of its reception of the ministry of Christ, and its provision for the representation in word and action of his ministry. The office is created as an expression of the continuing personal authority of Christ himself, and is dependent upon that authority.

But surely authority inheres in the person as well as the office, for where there is no actual ministry—and that means where there is no loving service—there the participation in the authority of Christ is obscured and may be lost. Both office and person become channels of grace through the concrete task of facing personal needs. It follows that to enter into the pastoral relationship involves, along with the assertion of authority, a risk and a search. New light on the Gospel and new self-discoveries are possible for both the pastor and the person who stands before him.

Some confirmations of this truth are so familiar that they need only be mentioned. We all know there is a difference between the authority with which the young seminary graduate begins his preaching and that of the pastor who has had years of experience of life and death among his people. There is authority in both cases. The untried young person may be wiser than the older one. He may quickly assert the authority of insight and spirit. But something must come slowly from the encounter with life and the testing which is brought by tragedy.

What needs our especial attention in this matter, however, is that every experience, with or without the high commission of the Church's ordination, opens the question of authority to interpret the Gospel. Every new problem and decision in the Christian life presents a new demand for the discovery of the real meaning of ministry.

A person may come to the minister with a question or problem which he has heard a hundred times, yet the question of the meaning of human existence is raised anew. To enter with any person into the search for the healing which the Gospel brings means to risk having one's understanding and one's faith challenged. We never know where a new human problem may lead us. This does not mean that the pastor is examining himself every five minutes to see whether he is establishing an authoritative relationship with his people. The point we are stressing here is perhaps quite rightly kept in the background most of the time. We have to go ahead and do what needs to be done, trusting in God's mercy and power. But when the question of authority to speak the words of forgiveness, of hope, and of judgment is decisively raised, we will discover that the crisis of authority is the crisis of faith itself. Without risking our very being in the service of Christ, we have no authority to speak in his name. We may rightly stress the positive aspect of this view of authority. The authentic power to be a pastor to another is born out of living encounters with those in need. God gives authority when we are open to his leading.

We should not oversimplify what is immensely complex and full of mystery. Pastoral authority has many dimensions: the tested experience of the pastor, the suffering out of which insight and strength are born, the knowledge of technical aspects of counseling and skill in dealing with human problems, all these play a part. There is the historical experience of the Church and the tradition of the pastoral office. No one ministers for himself alone. What is effective in any ministry is far more a power accumulated through centuries of experience than anything which we exercise as individuals. But tradition must finally take form in the personal actions of those who seek the healing power of God in present life.

A group of ministers in New York's East Harlem Protestant Parish, a significant church mission in a critical area of a great city, describes so exactly the discovery of authority through the act of ministry that it is appropriate to quote it here—all the more so since it deals with ministry to an entire community and not only to individuals.

In the beginning, the church was met with many signs of rejection and misunderstanding. Some thought it was a racket of the . . . congressman from the area. Others thought it was some kind of experiment or study project to investigate the people of the area. Sometimes the ministers were greeted with hostility or suspicion, although far more often with apathy, the incredible hopelessness about life that seemed to hang over so many of the people of East Harlem like a black cloud. In modern urban life, many people seem to have lost any sense of purpose or meaning in life; this was surely true in East Harlem. The problem for the young ministers, first of all, was to establish some kind of communication with East Harlem, to overcome the cultural barriers and get to know people at the level of our common humanity where the genuine religious issues arise. The key word became participation. They had so to share in the life of the community, to feel its concerns and pain, to face the same daily frustrations and tensions of urban life. The staff moved into tenement apartments, sought to meet people where they lived and played, to be on hand when trouble came, to listen and feel and wait. Gradually, over the early years, the ministers earned the right and opportunity through this kind of participation, to confront the people of East Harlem with the Gospel. Just as often, through sensitive and concerned members of the little colonies that began to grow, they were themselves ministered unto and inspired.[7]

Let us be clear that the final judgment as to what is authoritative in any Christian ministry and what is not, does not lie with us or with any human institution. It lies with God. Our world is full of claims to authority in matters of politics, of ethics, of the intellect, and of religion. We can pay our full respect to the tested structures of authority in our common life, but all conventional human authorities easily assume a finality beyond their competence, and this is nowhere more dangerously true than in the high forms of spiritual authority which belong to religion and its institutions.

V. THE HIDDENNESS OF MINISTRY

We began by stressing the public nature of the minister's authority. He presents, through his office and his vocation, the divine claim and gift to men. But the analysis of the actual content of that authority leads to the conclusion that there are two forms of exercise of ministerial authority, one public, and one hidden. If we do not see this, we will lack one of the main keys to understanding what happens in pastoral care, as well as miss some fundamental realities in the life and work of the Christian minister.

What we have to see is that the pastor not only embodies and uses the symbols of his public vocation, but that he has to learn to divest himself and his language at times of just these recognizable symbols in order to help people recover their real meaning. Most ministers at some time feel a deep need to become "anonymous" so that they can act as Christians without reference to their special vocation. There are many sources of this need, and one of them may be in the desire to escape the discipline involved. But at its deepest, this need stems from the realities of the Christian life. It is the need to get behind the veil of conventional symbols and forms to the quick of human life and experience. It is the protest against the misuse of sacred forms as escape from the real issues.

What all sensitive Christians feel here at some time about the danger of unreality in religious forms and symbols has received abundant confirmation in contemporary psychology. Religious symbols have an ambiguous power. For some people they become the main barriers between the self and reality. They function as bridges upon which we may walk to and fro from our private hurts to communicate with others, but never take a step off the bridge into a new way of life.[8]

For example, the great words and signs of grace and healing, such as forgiveness and love, may become the focus for resentment against other persons and life itself. The pastor who is trying to be helpful may become the surrogate for a parent who talked much of love and never understood it. The image of the Church may become inseparable from a class or caste, or from remembered injustice.

There is the further psychological insight that the person who uses religious language very freely, and who appears completely dependent on pious feelings and sentiments, may be concealing a profound disbelief in the very doctrines he aggressively affirms. Ambivalence in feelings is one of the first lessons the pastoral counselor must learn, and it raises many sharp questions about the meaning of pious observance.

We see, then, more clearly why the minister's office constitutes a special problem for him in many of his relationships even with his own congregation. There are always those Christians who have not reached enough maturity to discriminate between reality and form in religion. And we see why every minister will experience a sharp longing to exercise his vocation *incognito*.

Of course he cannot become completely divested of his public vocation; but he can know that for the sake of getting at realities he must become skilled in describing human problems in more than one language. We need not advocate the pastor's adoption of a completely secularized language in his counseling work. That is not an uncommon phenomenon; but surely it is a mistake. The Christian pastor has no adequate substitutes for the vocabulary which includes such words as "God," "faith," and "grace." Further, the use by either a pastor or a secular counselor of a profane and shocking vocabulary to exhibit his personal "release" is more a sign of lingering infantilism than of maturity. But the pastor may have to set aside all specifically religious language for a time precisely because at some stage of communicating with the person these get in the way of clear thought and honest feeling.

Take the term "sin," for example. There is no substitute for this word. There are analogues in "maladjustment," "egocentricity," "lack of integrity." But "sin" means man's

willful turning away from a loyal and trusting relationship
to God. It is a rupture at the center of the personal existence,
a rupture for which we in our freedom are responsible. It
is the self's flight from reality. Thus the word "sin" carries a
great freight of judgment and acknowledgment of wrong
with it. "For I acknowledge my transgressions: and my sin is
ever before me" (Ps. 51:3). This confession of the Psalmist
is at the center of the Christian experience. Yet no word in
our culture is more misused, misunderstood, and flagrantly
exploited than "sin," and none of us completely escapes the
distortion which it has undergone. Its religious and moral
depth has been flattened out to make it a suggestion merely
of the bad things people do, of unconventional behavior, or
failure in a purely legalistic morality. It is used to sell books
and moving pictures. At a more subtle psychological level it
becomes a useful word for those who do not really want to
change, and so they indulge in a continual "confession of
sin," replacing the will to change with the ritual of wallowing
in guilt.

The skillful counselor looks beneath the words and symbols
and finds ways to communicate around and through the blocks
which people may have about even the greatest words. It can
be truly said that the pastoral task is so to minister to people
who have lost the power of a right use of Christian language
that this language can be restored to them with reality and
with power.

What we are saying about the concealment of truth by
language is but one aspect of the ultimate truth about the
hiddenness of ministry. We are dealing here with the hiddenness of God himself. The Protestant Reformers rediscovered
what the New Testament declares, that in his revelation in
Jesus Christ God has expressed his love and at the same time
concealed his being. A strange ambiguity runs through the

Gospel record of Jesus. There are the signs of the Kingdom and of its power. These appear unmistakable. He taught as one having authority, and not as the scribes (Matt. 7:29). And yet none of the signs were really "unmistakable." It is possible to read the record and to remain, as many eyewitnesses were, quite unmoved by it. There is the important testimony in much of the Gospel record that Jesus disavowed all the common expectations of the power of Messiahship. He taught that the Messiah must suffer and die a human death. Here all the traditional signs and symbols break down. There is nothing left but the naked man upon the cross. The resurrection is indeed a sign of God's power, but it is surely not a public one. It was those who had lived within the orbit of the new faith who saw the resurrected Lord. After a brief period, Jesus "ascended to heaven," a clear indication that the presence of the resurrected Christ is a spiritual presence. We cannot say, "Lo here, and lo there," and point to the Kingdom. We can only say in the crises of life, "Surely the Lord was in this place." The Holy Spirit makes use of human and historical forms, but the Spirit bloweth where it listeth. God lends his presence through religious forms, but is not bound to them. The Scripture itself helps to protect us from a false faith in purely objective signs of authority. "Now we see through a glass, darkly; but then face to face." "Beloved, now are we the sons of God, and it doth not yet appear what we shall be." (I Cor. 13:12; I John 3:12.)

It has been the theme of this chapter that when we speak of authority in the Christian faith and ministry we must see that authority through its source in the revelation in Jesus Christ. This is to say that our authority derives from him whose claim rests finally on nothing other than the sheer expression of love to God and to men. We do not all agree in the Christian Church about the proper forms of authority in the ministry; but whatever they may be, we cannot escape the truth that God in his decisive word to us has left us no ultimate reliance upon institution or tradition save that which arises from personal trust in him.

In the next two chapters we shall discuss what happens when the pastor and another seek the healing power of grace in personal relationships.

CHAPTER 3

PERSONAL CHANNELS OF GRACE

We have examined the Christian understanding of salvation and the nature of the Christian ministry. We have seen the pastoral task as dependent upon the healing action of God, who redeems life for a new order beyond present guilt and fear. We have stressed that in the Christian view the saved and the healed life is given in responsible and loving service in the great task of world-making, and is not concerned merely to be relieved of private burdens.

We are now to give a more intensive examination to what happens when the individual comes to the pastor for help in time of trouble. While we concentrate on the individual person and his relationship to a counselor, we do not mean to forget the social dimension of life. Our problems are collective as well as individual. Personal peace or the lack of it is related to the threat of international war. Social problems can arise from individual maladjustments, and the amount of mental stress and psychological illness in itself constitutes a social problem. But here we focus our attention on the individual's search for meaning, for self-understanding, and for salvation. There is a sense in which every man stands alone before God. To the pastor come persons who at times are asking the final questions. They search for God.

We are asking what it is that can happen when a person

explores his problems intensively with another who is or becomes his pastor. We know that throughout the history of the Church such personal relationship has been one of the ways in which the power of God became manifest. There is Jesus' ministry of healing to sick people, some of them sick in mind as well as in body. There is the dramatic encounter with the woman at the well. The Christian Church has always conceived its ministry to be responsible for such personal communication and care.

If in the meeting of pastor and person what is done and said can open the way to healing or can block it, what makes the difference? It is the need to get further light on this question which has led in the twentieth century to a radical rethinking of the nature of pastoral care. There have been two main sources of that rethinking.

I. New Light on Personal Relationships

First, there is the new knowledge about the dynamics of personal relationships contributed by the depth psychology beginning with Freud. We do not forget how tentative are all the formulations of that knowledge. All of Freud's theories are criticized and many of them rejected by others. The whole field is in an exploratory stage. Yet we recognize that modern psychology has made us see personal relationships in a new light. The dynamics of human development, of sexual relationships, and of interpersonal adjustment are now interpreted with insights which have not been available in the past, and we have discovered that much pastoral work has been done in ignorance of many factors which we need to understand. Of course persons can be healed in spite of our inadequate knowledge of what is taking place. That is true now as always. It can be argued with evidence that some modern psychological theories have themselves become obstacles to understanding personal relationships. Notice the tendency

of psychologists to criticize their own methods in the light
of a more personal understanding of both counselor and
patient.[1] But we must not allow the routines of pastoral care
to go uncriticized, whether or not they have the prestige of
ecclesiastical authority and tradition behind them. I have
sat with groups of ministers in which all were given the
opportunity of reacting to personal problems brought before
the group, and have been with others shocked by the discovery
of how easily we fall into clichés of pastoral advice, and put a
person off from disclosing his real feelings. This is a salutary
experience for any pastor, and we owe its exploration in
considerable part to the work of the new psychology.[2]

The second source of the need to rethink pastoral counseling comes from theology. As we look at this mysterious
encounter between persons, we ask how the theological
interpretation of that relationship differs from the purely
psychological one. Does psychological healing take place
through human skill alone, or is there a dimension in it which
opens the way to a connection with the Christian understanding of grace? How does a person become a channel of grace?
What are the conditions, so far as we can state them, for the
empowerment which gives release to the person? Finally,
there arises the difficult question of what place is given to
the explicit acknowledgment in counseling of the religious
dimensions of life. Does something different take place when
the reality of God and his power are explicitly declared? What
about the healing which takes place when there is no such
acknowledgment?

In these questions we are at grips with the mystery of
grace itself. Theology is a reflection on what we can begin to
grasp of that mystery. If man is what the Christian faith believes him to be, then any account of personal growth and
healing which leaves the divine reality unacknowledged is
insufficient.

It is true that much of the psychological movement has been humanistically oriented and, with Freud himself, has tended to regard the religious dimension as illusory or at least as irrelevent to personal growth. Many, on scientific grounds, would like to restrict their horizon to the psychological structures which can be empirically recognized and to the skills which counselors develop in experience. Others like C. G. Jung in his Terry Lectures leave the way open to the religious interpretation "if we are so inclined," but seem to regard the question as irrelevant to the healing process.

Jung says:

> Nobody can know what the ultimate things are. We must, therefore, take them as we experience them. And if such experience helps to make your life healthier, more beautiful, more complete and more satisfactory to yourself and to those you love, you may safely say: "This was the grace of God."[3]

The reader of Jung's later book, *Answer to Job,* in which the psychologist makes the same disclaimer of any knowledge of an objective divine order, may well feel that in spite of this restriction, the meditation on God in that book shows that the question of the being and nature of God is inescapable in the depths of man's suffering.[4]

Now it is true that effective integration of human personality can take place under a variety of theories as to how it comes about. Health does not, fortunately, always depend upon our understanding of its sources. Further, we must agree that there are aspects of the Christian interpretation of life which never come directly into view in a psychological analysis. The relationship of the persons of the Trinity, for example, becomes a technical problem in Christian theology which may have little relevance to the person's search for God. But what the doctrine of the Trinity expresses concerning the place of love and freedom in God's being is highly pertinent to the meaning of God for man. The critical point is that *the interpretation of human experience is a constituent element in the experience.* Modern psychology has reinforced this point at every turn. Interpretation has played a central role in psychological theory since Freud's *Interpretation of Dreams.* It can be persuasively argued that here in this early work Freud expressed a more adequate anthropology than in his later more materialistic theory.[5] It has been acutely observed that Freudian patients under analysis tend to have, or at least to disclose, Freudian-type dreams, and that Jungian patients tend toward Jungian dreams, thus demonstrating how important language, symbols, and interpretation are to the personal life.

As we seek to understand man theologically, it is necessary to remember that any words which express thoughts and feelings may have theological or religious content. By the same token, we certainly do not eliminate the grace of God by failing to speak of it or to be aware of his presence.

II. A Study in Psychological Therapy

In order to give concreteness to our analysis of the religous aspect of experience, I introduce here a case study which has become publicly available and which has some universal aspects. Of course no single case can be taken to prove any point, but it can give us a basis for analysis. It is the case of Mrs. Oak, reported by Professor Carl Rogers as an example of the successful use of client-centered therapy at the research clinic which Dr. Rogers directed for many years at the University of Chicago.[6]

The salient facts are these: "Mrs. Oak" was a mother who came to the therapist in a state bordering on panic. Her relations with her daughter and been growing steadily worse. She felt unable to control her sexual feelings. The following description of her condition was given by the therapist at a stage early in the counseling period:

> She feels basically useless, formless, and is filled with anxiety and real fear, which she dares not face because of the "terrible things that lurk" beneath the surface. Her drive for achievement and high level aspiration are thus a type of "busy work"—a method of filling up her life with a lot of things about which she can feel or express concern even though she realizes they are rather unimportant. There is a great deal of compulsiveness in this busyness and a feeling of being driven by outside forces so that relaxation becomes impossible. . . . There are generalized suspicion, hostility, resentment, frustration, dejection, and strong guilt feelings directed specifically toward some family member . . . and considerable confusion about her own sex role. . . .
>
> Happiness to her is equivalent to lack of status (or desire for it), to relaxation, to having plenty of props to lean upon. Her guilt feelings are in large part related to denial of affectional responses, and to rebellion against outwardly imposed goals.[7]

The account of the conversations with the therapist are given in detail in the study. These are some of the high points:

Mrs. Oak discovers, when she begins to be able to express her real feelings, that she has been hurt "inside," and has not been able to admit it. At the same time she discovers that she is actually an interesting and comfortable person to be with, something she had not been able to feel or believe as her anxiety increased.

At one point she describes what is happening to her in the experience of self-discovery as the difference between ascending up in the air into a kind of thin ideal, which was what she had been trying to do, as over against the descent now into a solid reality. She needs to find a set of goals which represent her real being.

One of the critical moments comes when she discovers that it is important how the counselor feels about what may happen to her. Some especially important points about the function of the counselor are involved here. Mrs. Oak says (this is an exact transcription):

Well, I made a very remarkable discovery. I know it's. . . . I found out that you actually *care* how this thing goes. . . . It gave me a feeling, it's sort of well . . . maybe I'll let you get in the act, sort of thing. It's . . . again you see . . . it suddenly dawned on me that in the . . . client-counselor kind of thing you *actually care* what happens to this thing. And it was a revelation a . . . not that. That doesn't describe it. It was a . . . well . . . the closest I can come to it is a kind of relaxation, a . . . not letting down, but a . . . more of a kind of straightening out without tension if that means anything.[8]

One remarkable moment in the discovery of a new life comes when she walks out of the counseling session "knowing that she will never again need a father."[9]

Toward the end of the counseling, she describes the basis of the new life which has come to her (I slightly abridge the account):

She says: "It's based on something pretty doggoned deep, a—a feeling that (pause) sort of that from here on in I'm sort of going to have to play the thing on my own, with my own ship. And . . . I'm scared." (Pause)

Coun. "It seems a slightly lonesome and risky affair."

She replies that it is, but this loneliness is herself and she has to accept it or "it wouldn't be me."

Coun. "So that the loneliness which comes from being you, you'll take and, you wouldn't trade it for anything."

She replies that this is true and that she faces life "not knowing she is going to win," and the counselor says, "and yet you wouldn't back out of it."

She says: "I—it seems to me the only thing I can think of is—

is . . . St. Matthew said it I think, "rejoice and be exceedingly glad that. . . ."

The counselor asks if this means rejoicing in something negative; she replies:

"No, it isn't negative . . . I don't know, I mean . . . the only kind of imagery I can bring into the thing, is—is a feeling sometimes of—of walking through life, with the whole goddamn world just kind of—of going to . . . pieces, and—and kind of picking my way, and still this sense of—of 'rejoice and be exceedingly glad.' So, I suppose there is . . the element of the thing being negative."[10]

Here are the summarizing statements of the counselor as to what has happened:

1. The essence of this process is not that certain *content* material is admitted to awareness, but that the client discovers that recognizing an experience for what it *is* constitutes a more effective method of meeting life than does the denial or distortion of experience. . . .

2. The client discovers that what has been needed is a love which is not possessive, which demands no personal gratification.

3. There is the discovery that there is, at the core of one's being, nothing dire or destructive of self, and nothing damaging or possessive or warping of others.

4. The client comes to feel that it is possible to walk with serenity through a world that seems falling to pieces.[11]

We readily see some of the ways in which this case reveals universal elements in our experience, and significant aspects of the restoration to mental health. The case is remarkable, not only for what is said by client and counselor, but also because of what they do not say. There is little explicit discussion of religious issues. The counselor seems definitely to keep them to one side. Mrs. Oak's language at times touches upon religious confession, as in the striking quotation from

the Gospel of St. Matthew. This is significant not only because it is a biblical text, but because it seems for her to sum
up in a decisive way the meaning of her self-discovery. But
for the most part, the issues dealt with do not seem to take
the form of theological questions about the meaning of life.
Attention is focused on this one person's inner struggle, on
her immediate feelings and relationships. And the outcome
seems to be stated as an inward reorganization and recovery,
not as a new structure of religious belief. Nothing is said
about God.

Nothing is said either about ethical obligation in the new
life. The statement about the "love which is not possessive"
certainly has ethical implications, but there is, for instance,
no raising of the question as to how Mrs. Oak will now deal
with issues of social justice. Is one who has been through this
kind of self-discovery necessarily more sensitive to the larger
ethical obligation beyond the family? This question must
surely be asked when we look at counseling from any ethical
point of view, let alone that of the Christian faith.

When we raise these questions it is not to suggest that the
counseling of this distressed person should have proceeded
as a discussion of the theological and ethical issues. In a great
many cases the immediate discussion of these questions would
only get in the way of the real discovery of the self. But what
we do insist upon is that in the final analysis of any human
problem, we have to raise these ultimate religious questions if
we are to have any adequate understanding of what fulfills
a human life. It is difficult indeed to know when and how in
the midst of our anxieties and fears we can think truly about
the meaning of God and our relationship to our neighbor.
Just here we need some careful theological discrimination in
our understanding of the pastoral task.

I suggest that we need to recognize what we have called
in the first chapter the principle of "linkage" in experience.

Wherever we begin with human problems we recognize that what we see and feel here and now may break open for us at any time questions concerning the meaning of our existence. And the question of the meaning of "my" existence leads surely to the question of the meaning of all existence. I cannot understand one without the other. But if this be true, then the introduction of the question about God into the search for personal healing is not arbitrary. It is the root question which underlies every other question.

III. The Self-Image

Let us explore, then, this religious dimension of experience by analyzing a concept which is common to all contemporary psychology, the "self-image."

Every person has a way in which he sees himself in relation to others, a "self-image." The "image" is not something exclusively or even primarily intellectual, sharply defined, and fully present to consciousness. It is not without structure, for as we begin to explore it consciously we often discover its sources and its outlines with disturbing clarity; but only in rare moments is this structure consciously outlined before us. It is constituted by our feelings about ourselves, and others' feelings about us as we have taken those feelings into ourselves. It includes our sense of our role in life, our capacities, and our inferiorities. It includes our ideals, and may take the form of an ideal image of the self which is in sharp contrast to the real image, that is, how we "really" feel about ourselves. We know that the image in all its aspects carries a heavy emotional charge. Threats to our self-image are felt as threats to our very being. In a sense they are really that, for our being includes this self-interpretation of what we are.

We know that one of the important things that happen in the therapy of counseling is that we are able to get our self-image out before us so that we can see it for what it is. If there is a discrepancy between the ideal and the actual self-image, we can become aware of it. What is false in the self-image, that is, what does not accord with our knowledge or sense of reality, what is intolerably beyond our power to sustain, what has been created in order to protect us from hurts, and what reflects our genuine self—all this can in a measure be brought into the light of a new judgment. This reordering of the self-image is a fundamental aspect of our growth into maturity.

We have now to ask about the place of the counselor in this process of bringing the self-image to light. We all know that "talking it out" with an understanding person can help. We know more clearly now that it is important for that person to be one in whose presence we are not afraid to disclose ourselves, and one who will listen patiently for what we really are seeking to disclose. When these conditions are fulfilled, healing is more likely.

How does healing come? Why is it not easier to face ourselves when we are alone and need fear no judgment from someone else? Why is it so difficult to face ourselves alone, and what is this need to have another to whom we can tell what needs to be told? These questions put us on the track of the dynamics of change in the self.

Some of the counselor's functions are obvious. He is someone to talk to, so that we can hear what we say as a communication to another person. The counselor may help to interpret what we say, and his questions may help us to come out with it. But these elements are not the whole. The deeper truth, as Freud discovered, is that there is something in the personal relationship being established which has power to release the self and lead to self-understanding. Freud says in his *General Lectures on Psychoanalysis* (the first version of those lectures):

The outcome in this struggle is not decided by his [the patient's] intellectual insight . . . it is neither strong enough nor free enough to accomplish such a thing, but solely by his relationship to the physician.[12]

We see this truth illustrated in the case of Mrs. Oak. One of the decisive disclosures in the case is her testimony that the crux of the healing process was her discovery one day that the counselor really cared about her finding her way through. Much attention is being given to this aspect of the counseling situation. Existential psychotherapy has as one of its special emphases the counselor's active role in venturing upon a real personal relationship where feelings must be disclosed on both sides.

Freud supplied a major insight into the dynamics of this relationship in his discovery of the "transference." "A patient can be influenced only so far as he invests objects with *libido*."[13] What happens, in Freudian theory, is that the natural love power becomes frustrated and is not creatively expressed because of the fears and inhibitions which arise in the infantile situation. The counselor provides a new object for the expression of the *libido,* an object who is a person who will not reject the struggling self. The patient can, so to speak, discharge both his love and his hostility upon the counselor and this has power to objectify these profound feelings. In time this relationship becomes a transition stage toward the patient's discovery of an adequate object of his love, and one in accordance with reality. I am aware that there are many complexities in the transference, and that the client-centered therapists have rejected the Freudian emphasis upon it. But the point that the counselor enters into a relationship in which the emotional factors of the client's attitude toward him are of basic importance is one upon which psychological theories agree.

So far, then, we see how the self-image can be objectified in the personal relationship where it can be both fully acknowledged and transformed. We need not pursue the technical description of this process further, important as its aspects are to a full theory of counseling. Our theological concern leads now to the proposal that all interpretation of the self-image and its transformation is incomplete, and in a sense misleading, unless we recognize the dimension of the search for the real world.

The religious question is inescapable in an adequate theory of the self-image. Let us return to the experience of Mrs. Oak for a clue. There is an interesting remark in an early interview in which she speaks about the daughter with whom she is having so much trouble. The daughter represents the real world which must be met, and the relation to her involves the meaning of the mother's life. She says of the daughter, "I have made this girl my only link with life."[14]

We see that the self-image is never *only* a self-image, it is an understanding of life. What the self is seeking within itself can never be found apart from the finding of reality beyond the self. We know who we are and what we are when we discover what we belong to. I do not mean that we are always occupied with metaphysical reflection when we think about ourselves. I mean that in the depth of our self-searching we cannot avoid coming upon the ultimate religious questions: What is life? Why are we born? What does it mean that we learn to love and care for life and then we die? What makes all the pain and struggle worth while, if anything does?

When we see that there can be no self-understanding apart from some grasp of Origin and Destiny, an understanding which certainly includes an acknowledgment of what is unknown in both Origin and Destiny, then the counselor with whom we seek self-understanding takes on a new significance. He is there, not only as trained physician, or professional psychologist, or as ecclesiastically authorized pastor. He represents that world with which the person must come to terms. He is the bearer of some truth about life which must be grasped, because to lose it is to lose everything. And this may be so even when the counselor himself is not aware of what he means to the searching person before him.

We will miss the point of this view of the counselor if we try to conceive his role primarily in relation to his conscious analysis of the patient's problems. All that is important, but the counselor is not related to a patient primarily as an illustration of a general principle or as an oracle of wisdom. Indeed we know that where the patient thinks of the counselor in this way some necessary elements in the healing situation are lacking. It is vital for the pastor to realize how strong and pervasive the positive and negative attitudes toward the pastoral office may be, often in the same person. What we are pointing out is that every deep personal relationship is set in a context where each person is continually being moved to turn his attention to the reality which stands over against and between the persons. When someone comes to a counselor for help, he is searching for some reason to go on living. Unless there is some hope, and some new possibility beyond the present struggle, there is no reason for his coming. As William Ernest Hocking has remarked, if the counselor sees no meaning for living, then he is the one who is in need of help, whatever is to be said of the person who comes to him.[15]

In the case of Mrs. Oak there occurs a poignant disclosure of this significance of the counselor in something she says after the interviews have led her a long way toward a new life. She says to him, "You are my love." This statement is not sentimentality, but the strictest realism. She has begun to discover the solid substance of her own being in this possibility of love which is incarnate in the other person. He has, for the moment, become the focus of reality without which she cannot live.

Say then that human relationships are never dyadic, but always triadic. There is a reality which stands *between* the persons, and that reality, to keep our terms neutral for the moment, is the meaning of existence as it really is. It is what sets the bounds and establishes the possibilities of our being. When Mrs. Oak comes to the resolution of her problem, we recall, she speaks in religious terms. The new way means to "rejoice and be exceedingly glad" with the world going to pieces. She identifies this as "mystical" experience, without elaborating any theological explanation of it. But we see that what has taken place has been a transaction not only between herself and the counselor, but with a reality which is neither of them, nor the two together, but that which holds, measures, and justifies them in one world of meaning.

IV. CHRIST—THE MAN BETWEEN

We shall now give a theological interpretation of the counseling relationship which goes beyond what psychology can affirm. What we have said so far about the structure of the self-image is, I believe, truth which can be discovered in every psychological inquiry into the nature of the self. Rollo May has put us particularly in his debt by his insistence that an "ontology of human existence" is required even with the strict limits of psychological theory.[16] But now we go beyond the general doctrine of man to the Christian answer to the religious question. Our interpretation of the self-image becomes theological when we speak from within the faith of the Church and say that the objective reality which stands between persons is God made personal and available to us in Jesus Christ. What men seek is what can make life whole. It must be reality present to us as truth and as power. That is,

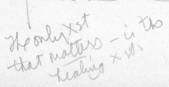

what men are really searching for is the Christ, the personal
presence of God in human life.

Our question about the Christ, we see, has a double aspect.
On the one hand, we seek a true knowledge of what we are.
Christ is the person who discloses us to ourselves. On the
other hand, he is the New Man, the one who opens the way
to what we can become. He is one of us, tempted in all points
as we are, yet he bears the courage and love which can transform us. It is Christ who is the Third Man in every human
relationship.

Consider three aspects of this view of how we know ourselves through Christ.

First, there is the Christian understanding of the mode
of our knowledge of God. It is his personal disclosure in
human life which establishes our knowledge of him and of
ourselves. God is more than pure form or abstract principle.
He is the One who calls us into personal communion with
him. We must indeed be careful in using personal symbols
for God. They can be so reduced to finite dimensions that they
lose their significance even for expressing our personal relationship to him. Tillich rightly warns us:

The criticism by psychology and sociology of personalistic
symbols for man's relation to God must be taken seriously by
theologians. It must be acknowledged that the two central symbols, Lord and Father, are stumbling blocks for many people
because theologians and preachers have been unwilling to listen
to the often shocking insights into psychological consequences
of the traditional use of these symbols.[17]

To say that God is personal for us in Jesus Christ does not
eliminate the mystery of the Father's being. What we know
in Jesus Christ is that God loves us in a way which is reflected
in, but transcends, our human understanding. St. Paul says
that it is only at the end that we will know as we are known.

thus asserting both our personal knowledge of God and the limits of that knowledge (I Cor. 13:12).

Second, to see Christ as the Third Man relating each man to his neighbor and to God is to say that human history is the story of the fall from a loving relationship into the actual estrangement of sin and its consequences. We see those consequences beating upon the Christ in the story of his life and death. In Paul's daring word, "God . . . made him to be sin who knew no sin" (II Cor. 5:21). What the New Testament requires of us is an acknowledgment of the distortion which sin produces in man's understanding of himself. Think of the ways in which the name and authority of Jesus have been used to justify every sort of human cruelty. Christians do not all see Christ in the same way. The story of the New Testament should remind us that even our knowledge of him bears the marks of our distorted self-images, which always threaten to separate us from others. Somerset Maugham, who certainly has no theological ax to grind, could be documenting the doctrine of original sin in psychological terms when he writes:

When we come to judge others, it is not by ourselves that we judge them, but by an image that we have formed of ourselves from which we have left out everything that offends our vanity or would discredit us in the eyes of the world.[18]

The relation to Christ should bring a continual correction of our self-images.

In the third place, to see Christ as the reality which stands between man and man means that there is given to each life the possibility of a new way which involves a restoration to our right mind and the freedom to become a new person.

One of the important discoveries in the experience of counseling is that for a person to begin the search for himself is like facing death. In one sense it is that quite literally, the death of that self-interpretation which he has lived upon and cherished through the years. Now it is threatened. If it crumbles, he faces the world with no supports. This is a shattering and ofttimes terrifying experience. Anyone who has been there knows.

We need not be surprised, therefore, that the biblical words of death and resurrection occur quite readily to the pastor in thinking about the care of souls. The new life in Christ is the discovery of a new self on the other side of an old existence which must be let go.

True, the Christian symbol of resurrection is associated directly with immortality, that is, with life beyond physical death, but we should not forget that the Apostle Paul and the Fourth Evangelist see much more in it. "Reckon ye also yourselves to be dead unto sin, but alive unto God . . ." (Rom. 6:11). "You died, and your life is hid with Christ in God" (Col. 3:3). "This is life eternal, that they might know thee the only true God, and Jesus Christ, whom thou hast sent" (John 17:3). These are assertions of the resurrected life as present experience. They anticipate the immortality of participation in the love of God, but they begin now with a new life in which sin has been exposed and we have been reconciled.

We have been seeking to understand the structure of human life as a history of personal relationships in which God's grace works as transforming power. God's grace is his love in action.[19] To have some insight into the conditions through which God works is in no way to achieve control over grace. It is only to see a little way into the situation, and to enable us at times to keep from obstructing God's working. We know very little about the conditions which determine how God may work with us, and we cannot set limits to his working under any conditions. But we do know that the spirit of loyalty to other persons, of openness to being transformed ourselves, and a willingness to endure the pain of risking ourselves in the search for the truth, are among those conditions.

I must guard against one possible misunderstanding of the position here taken. By asserting this Christological interpretation of the pastoral relationship, one might seem to be offering an alternative to that patient exploration of the specific problems and emotional patterns of people's lives which psychiatrists and other counselors carry on. But this would be a gross misunderstanding of the position. I propose no substitution of piety for psychiatry. Let us keep our theological sights clean. Jesus Christ entered fully into our humanity. He took it all, with its endless complexities and problems, upon himself. He offered no simple way out. What he offered was the spirit of love acting in self-identification with human needs. Therefore, wherever we are honestly probing for reality, with psychological instruments or others, Christ is already present. The Christian pastor will find nothing alien to his concern in any human experience, in so far as his limitations of skill and human insight will permit. When psychologists speak of "regression in the service of the ego," they are describing the return to the primitive and elemental roots of personal development as the way to discovering and affirming our real selves. The pastor does not try to avoid this process. He is not there just to help a person "scale the heights"; he is there to walk with him in the valley of the shadow of death, for Christ has walked there before ever we did. What this means in facing the darker aspects of human experience we shall see in the next chapter.

CHAPTER 4

Atonement in counseling

FORGIVENESS, JUDGMENT,
AND ACCEPTANCE

The Counselor's Christology

We have offered a Christological interpretation of personal relationships. When a broken self finds healing and strength, the healing power belongs neither to the self nor to another who acts as psychiatrist or pastor. It belongs to a power operative in their relationship. That power is God, who as we know him in the Christian faith, is revealed to us in Jesus Christ, the Third Man, who discloses the truth about our humanity in its need and in its hope.

Christian affirmation about the work of Christ in transforming men is interpreted in the doctrines of atonement. God has given his son to die for us, and through him the grace of forgiveness has become the redemptive power in life. I propose now to ask whether some light on the meaning of atonement may come from the new perspectives in pastoral care. None of the traditional doctrines of atonement has been quite satisfying to the Church or to Christian faith. We cannot replace those traditional theories. They all reflect aspects of the truth. But we can, I believe, get further light on what they try to say by giving attention to the personal experience of forgiveness and renewal.

We are dealing here with the very difficult questions of the relation of psychological concepts of healing to ultimate affirmations of faith in God and his grace. Therefore, it will be well to begin our analysis by setting alongside each other two accounts of release from the burden of guilt, one theological and one psychological. Then we can ask what light they may throw upon each other.

I. GRACE AS FORGIVENESS

To begin with the theological account: in the Christian faith every self bears both the dignity and the risks of freedom. As creature the self stands before the Creator, not with an unqualified freedom, but with a margin of personal response. We are free to love God and our neighbor, and such love is perfect freedom for it is the fulfillment of our being. But in our freedom we may violate the spirit of love. We may resist our own fulfillment. Every self does.

There is a history of sin, which, in Christian faith, is always misused freedom. It is a history in which all are involved, and it is a history for each individual, for so long as we are human we are never completely dominated by the social group. The story of sin is the course which the soul runs as it turns away from life with God and his love, and seeks life on terms of its own making. The three classic descriptions of the root sin all throw light upon it. They are: unbelief, or lack of trust in God; *hybris,* man's elevation of himself as usurper of God's place; and concupiscence, the turning of the self upon itself to feed upon its own gratifications. Sin is violation of our essential nature, therefore it always results in a state of inner dividedness. We are at war with ourselves as well as with God. Here is the theological understanding of why men turn to a deceitful self-glorification or to self-destruction. We defy God by asserting our own power and goodness as absolute, or we try to flee from ourselves.

This analysis helps to explain why much self-glorification conceals an element of self-destruction. We must hide the truth that we are not so strong or self-sufficient as we profess. This concealment may be very deep, and it is greatly reinforced by collective pride. Reinhold Niebuhr has depicted so well the way in which both our individual pride and our individual weakness may find compensation in glorifying the power and virtue of the group to which we belong. Yet the element of self-rejection in sin will usually be found if we dig deeply enough. And to complete the dialectic, this very self-rejection may draw strength from a defiance of life and God. One of John Barrymore's friends, discussing the great actor's behavior in his last years, said,

> And I wish to tell you now that my opinion of his character . . . is this: When he sneered at and abused himself beyond the tolerance of the crowd, it was not done through weakness but through strength, a defiance of God.[1]

The Christian description of this divided self has always used the image of the self's bondage, without losing sight of the truth that this bondage is guilt. We are responsible, yet we become helpless to extricate ourselves from the maelstrom of our distorted selfhood. Let us not accept this assertion of the reality of man's guilt as something obvious. There are great perplexities here. There is, for one thing, the variety of human experience. There is the history of each life as it is influenced by other lives, and the fact of our mutual involvement in destructive action. If, for example, we are dealing with a juvenile delinquent, at what point are we to see this fourteen-year-old boy as responsible in spite of the social misery and disorder or family disintegration in which his life may be lived? Who is delinquent? Parents, society, or the individual? Again, we must see that sin is a corruption at the root of our being, if we are to have any right understanding of it. What we call "sins," particular wrong actions, are for the most part to be understood as symptoms of the fundamental disorder which lies deep in the spirit.

It is of critical importance when we interpret sin that we keep our affirmation of real guilt and our high view of man together. In the Christian faith, so long as we are real persons we are never wholly at the mercy of our neuroses or maladjustments or purely external influences. Real guilt is the obverse side of the dignity of freedom. An important part of self-clarification is the clear acceptance of personal responsibility, not only for the future, but for the whole of one's life. To shoulder this responsibility and yet to recognize how our freedom is qualified by what we cannot control is a delicate and important aspect of the struggle for maturity.

The Christian Gospel, the Good News, is that there is a way through the bondage of the self. Although we can find neither the insight nor the will to escape, God has come to us from beyond ourselves to break up our ill-founded self-assurance, and our despair. He has disclosed his forgiveness and his healing power. We can be restored to our rightful minds. It is this action of God which has come to its decisive climax in the story of Jesus, in whom he has opened the way for us. God in his love has come where we are, and walked the tragic, hate-ridden paths of human history. He took the consequences of sin upon himself in loneliness, sweat, and anguish. Jesus is the man of God, standing loyally by the Father's purpose, and loyally by the Father's children, who have lost their way. It is in Jesus' giving of himself that we begin to know in depth what God's grace truly is. So we speak of his action in Jesus Christ as the atonement for our sin. Through what he has done, reconciled men can begin to live a new life and love one another as God has loved them.

The traditional theories of the atonement all attempt some accounting of this supreme mystery of grace. Each grasps some aspect of the truth, the ransom theory, the debt of honor theory, the moral influence theory, but none exhausts it. Even to mention them is to recognize how long and inconclusive the discussion has been. It is noteworthy that the Christian Church has never arrived at one ecumenical and orthodox statement of the meaning of the atonement. It is as if the reality is such that it stubbornly refuses to be confined in a doctrine. Yet all the theories hold that there is given to us from beyond ourselves a new relationship to God which empowers us to live in a new way. This power is grace. It does not come in the first instance as a summons to take heart, and to gird up our moral wills, but rather as an invitation to confess our inability to release ourselves from bondage, a call to open ourselves to a love which is freely given, which has never let us go, and which is ours on the sole condition that we are willing to trust the God who so loves us.

II. The Psychological Account of Personal Release

After this brief statement of the Christian account of reconciliation of the self we turn to the psychological account of the frustrated personality and the way to its release. Here we find a story which runs with a certain analogy to the Christian account of sin and the new life. Let us tell it also briefly before we ask how far these two views may be related to each other.

The theme of the self's inner conflict and its bondage to powers which cannot be broken by effort appears again in the psychological story of mental illness. What happens is that the freedom of the self and its power to maintain a basic integrity of thought and feeling are disrupted. It is as if the natural growth of the person has become blocked. The accounts of this blocking range all the way from Freud's theory of the *oedipus complex* to Jung's theory of the splitting off of the conscious life from its integration with its creative source in the one great stream of psychic life which has its major symbols or archetypes of meaning.[2]

The blocking of the self from its potential growth manifests itself in the sick personality as a loss of "self-possession." There is unresolved inner conflict. The person cannot handle his emotional life. He builds increasing defenses against the world outside and against admitting his real state. His condition can indeed be described as a kind of bondage, for a part of the personality appears to take over for the whole. We say he "acts compulsively," or that he "loses objectivity." Anxiety functions no longer as a creative awareness of danger, but as a destructive force sweeping away intelligent self-direction.

To be sure, there are many kinds of psychic illness, and much that is still completely baffling about them. And where something is known about how the therapy of personal counseling may help, there is still much we do not know about how this happens. But some of the essentials of healing through personal counseling are known. There is the presence of a psychiatrist or pastor, or some other person to whom we can speak about the feelings and fears which are the symptoms of our unrest, and perhaps ultimately we can begin to speak about those things which are the roots of our anxiety. This requires a patient exploration of the recesses of experience, both past and present. It is a reliving of what we have been as we search for a new interpretation of what it means. When this searching takes place in an atmosphere which does not threaten the person with rejection, no matter what he may disclose; when there is the wisdom and technical knowledge required to help the person to a new interpretation; and above all, when the counselor is able to communicate his own willingness to enter with this person into the new orientation toward which he is moving, there can take place (certainly it does not always happen) a reorganization of the personality. Hidden strengths in the self appear. Those things which have masked the real person are stripped off. The power to shape one's own life is reasserted. We say that the self has become free.

In all such accounts of psychological therapy there is overwhelming evidence that the ability of the counselor in some way to become a means of the self-expression for the other is of crucial importance, and that means the counselor's ability to take the feelings of the other sympathetically into his own being. It is this "taking in of the feelings of the other" to which we usually refer as psychological "acceptance."

We should say at once that "permissiveness" is not an adequate word for the attitude we are examining. Permissiveness rightly connotes a withholding of judgment, and that is part of the meaning of acceptance, but only a part. Acceptance is a positive process. It is not a passive taking in of another's problems, but a deliberate and constructive act of self-identification.

III. The Relation of Psychology and Theology

Now are we talking about the same thing when we speak of grace and forgiveness in Christian terms and acceptance in psychological terms? Are these two entirely different aspects of human experience, or are they the same thing described in different languages, or are there relationships and analogies between the two while they yet remain two? I shall take the third view of the matter, but before I state my reasons it will be well to look at the case for the view that the two perspectives are completely different. We are here at the heart of the problem of how Christian faith is related to psychology, and it is necessary to analyze carefully what is involved.

There are three main arguments for keeping the theological account of grace and the psychological account of "acceptance" quite separate. First, it may be said that the transaction between the guilty soul and God is not the same as the encounter, however profound it may be, between two persons who are concentrating on a personal problem and are not asking questions about man's guilt or responsibility before his Creator. Paul Tillich, who has done so much to clarify the relationship between theology and psychiatry, rightly insists that the religious dimension of healing is related to, but goes beyond, the cure of particular neuroses.[3] What Tillich calls "ontological anxiety" and "personal guilt" arise within man's "ultimate concern." They involve every man in his freedom before God. They cannot be removed by any readjustment of particular psychological structures.

Second, there is the point that the grace of forgiveness involves the confession of actual personal guilt. Where there is no guilt, forgiveness is meaningless. Guilt involves a personal alienation from God and the neighbor for which we are responsible. This responsibility may be shared, but it cannot be escaped. To deny it is to reject the Christian understanding of what it means to be human. We may find it instructive that in human relations forgiveness always threatens to become a kind of weapon which men use against one another, for the very act of forgiveness implies a judgment. This is why we have a natural resentment of being forgiven, with its implication of moral superiority in the other. We know it is only mutual forgiveness which can keep human efforts at reconciliation from becoming destructive.

When, therefore, we do confess our need for the forgiveness of God, we acknowledge our guilt. There can be no question of avoidance of judgment against us; the judgment is there in the very act of reconciliation. But does acceptance in psychological terms require such a personal acknowledgment of guilt before God, or even guilt in relation to other persons? This is a fair question. In the last analysis I believe acceptance does require this, but it must be admitted that some psychological theories keep the dimension of personal guilt in the background, and some have at times appeared to deny it altogether. It is not obvious that the ultimate responsibility of man is acknowledged in psychological therapy. We must look deeply if we are to find it.

The third point is that for Christian faith the healing of the soul comes from beyond the person and the counselor. It is God who heals, working beyond all human resources. I have argued in the preceding chapter that every personal relationship lifts our eyes toward a reality which transcends man. But even if this be acknowledged, surely, some will say, when we speak of the personal grace of forgiveness, we are going far beyond what can be documented in any psychological account of therapy. Grace means the way in which God deals with our human condition, his active purpose for the creation, his power to redeem and save history from its bloody tragedy, his offer of eternal life. None of this perspective of faith need be introduced in order to give an adequate empirical account of the release of the frustrated ego. Indeed, do we not need to explain the fact that many sick persons will be positively harmed if they are confronted with the sheer declaration of God's judgment and his forgiveness? The neurotic syndrome may include a deep anxiety about these very affirmations. The religious discussion of guilt may prevent a person from taking a first step toward dealing with his personal guilt feelings. His repressed guilt may be too shattering to be borne without a long preparation in the accepting situation. Would we not therefore do better to keep the ultimate structure of grace and forgiveness quite apart from the medical and psychological problems peculiar to certain persons?

I have put the case here as strongly as possible because it is a great danger to the concerns both of religion and of psychology to give a glib and simple interpretation of their relationship. We do no service to the care of souls by being vague in our language through a desire to "bring us all together." Having said this, I must go on to contend that we cannot keep these two accounts of human experience wholly separate. They involve each other, and taken together they give light which both theology and psychology need. The mystery of atonement can be approached with new understanding if theology and psychology will look together at the same reality, however difficult it may be to do so.

IV. The Meaning of Acceptance

I propose to examine more closely the meaning of "acceptance" as a term which both psychiatry and theology may use in describing the release of the self from its bondage.

Begin with the question "Who is accepted?" It is customary to say, "The whole person is accepted," with all his limitations and strengths, his hostilities and his love. Acceptance does have this dimension of "completeness." No one who has heard Charlotte Elliot's hymn, "Just as I am, without one plea," in a serious religious setting can mistake its power which rests upon a profound psychological as well as theological truth. The self makes no pretense. It is offered, "just as I am." But who is this "I"? We must look more closely at the self.

Karen Horney in her book, *Neurosis and Human Growth*, distinguishes three aspects of the self. There is an empirical or actual self, an ideal self, and the real self.[4] None of these selves completely includes the others. They overlap, but there is tension among them. The empirical self is that which we have become through the experiences of life. It is the self which others immediately begin to know, and which in a sense we know as "ourselves." It is what I recognize as being "me."

The ideal self is, in one sense, an aspect of the empirical self, for the ideal self has in large part also been born out of experience. It is our picture of what we aspire to be, our projection of what we believe would be the fulfillment of our lives. We have this ideal self in part confused with our actual self in the sense that we see ourselves through the glass of our own ideals. At the same time, we may feel a great discrepancy between the actual and the ideal. Our ideal may function as the law and judgment which we use against ourselves. It is far from what we actually are and usually we know this. Both these selves are operative aspects of the personality. What then is the real self?

In this analysis the real self is largely the *potential* of the personality. It is that which we truly can become if we are released from the distortion of our own false judgments, and from the blocking of our power to grow. The real self, therefore, is never identical with the actual self, for it is always more than we are at any moment of life. The real self is becoming. As Hocking says, "the self is a hope."[5]

The real self and the ideal self are never identical, for our true potential is something discovered in the course of life, and when discovered it comes as a judgment upon the ideal we have projected. We find who we really are only by "living life out." In this view we explicitly reject the notion, often quite heroically held, that we can by effort of will make ourselves adequate to the ideals we accept. There will always be discrepancy. Our very effort betrays us. The psychological clinical materials are full of the disastrous consequences of trying to fit life to a rigid ideal.

Now the point of this analysis is that when we ask *what self is accepted* in therapy, the answer must be that all these selves are accepted, but in somewhat different senses. The actual self is accepted. This is the primary condition of all successful therapy. The actual self is accepted in the sense that the person is allowed to express himself, his feelings, his fears, and his hopes as they are. The actual self is not accepted for the sake of the ideals which the person professes. Indeed, it is not accepted for the sake of the real self, the potential self, but "just as the person is," he is received, without rejection, without shock, and with understanding. Let us stress that this initial acceptance is not based upon the fact that this person represents a "type of psychological problem," or is to be seen as a case for experimentation. All this may be in the professional counselor's mind, but it cannot be determinative, else the person will know that he is not being accepted for himself.

The ideal self is accepted also. There are subtleties here. The self-ideal is a part of the person. He holds a certain picture of himself as he ought to be or might be. But the ideal self is not to be accepted in the sense that it defines the real good of the person. This is of critical importance, and just here much well-intentioned pastoral counseling fails. Out of religious and moral conviction we tend to praise people for their high intentions, and to sympathize with their sense of inability to live up to the ideals they hold. It seems so much like the confession of sin before the righteousness of God. It may be nothing of the sort. It may mean only that the real self is being smothered by an unexamined conflict between actual and ideal. The counselor and pastor must know that the ideal self is in some respects always a deformation of the person. It has been born in part out of the failure to achieve a decisive integration. We cannot deny that there is a problem here for Christian faith. The conflict between the law in the mind and that in the members, of which St. Paul speaks, is real and inescapable; but the point is that we should not confuse our self-imposed distortions of the "law of the mind" with the law of God. At this point in the care of the soul we encounter a profound and perennial problem, the relation of the law and the Gospel.

The real self also is to be accepted. It is this point which even some psychological theory seems to overlook. If there is no real self which is struggling to be born, there is no point to the therapeutic process. The person must literally come to know who he really is, and his real being is, for the most part, beyond his own sight and that of his counselor.

We need not fall into the error of idealizing this real self. It is the free person, God's creature, facing the ultimate issues of life and death, but facing them in their final dimensions, and making decisions which arise from the creative courage of one who has faced and accepted the conditions of real life.

We have come far enough to see that acceptance is a creative process. The criticism of psychological acceptance which some theologians have raised seems to me to overlook what actually happens in the counseling process.[6] To accept another person means to enter into this struggle of the self to be born anew. It requires, therefore, a positive and outgoing action of the counselor. The process has indeed a destructive side, for so much of what passes for the communication of persons in superficial living must now give way to the painful process of exploring what is hard to admit, and the giving up of cherished self-images. But this destruction is for the sake of reconstruction.

That this is what acceptance involves is amply supported by the evidence from counseling experience. Consider the fact that to be accepted requires courage. Tillich has written of the courage to accept acceptance as essential in the life of faith.[7] This courage appears in the therapeutic situation. One of Freud's startling discoveries was that persons will resist the very accomplishment of the release which therapy is achieving. We fear that which we desperately need. The root of this resistance lies in part in the superego, with its threat to whatever separates the person from his emotional attachments to the parent. But beyond this is the risk of becoming a new self. This is threatening because the new is untried, unknown. We fear that we will not recognize ourselves, so we cling to our familiar though painful paths. Psychiatrists sometimes express amazement that people are willing to suffer so much and so needlessly. There may be a partial explanation in the masochistic structure, but I believe there is a more fundamental reason. It is the stubborn, misguided fight for self-preservation. We have a metaphysical and religious need to *know who we are*. The venture of self-acceptance and being accepted by another threatens our present picture of who we are. When we understand this, we begin to see the radical character of acceptance, and to see that it does touch the ultimate meaning of life with which religion is concerned.

Let us go on then to the question: "Who is it who accepts?" There are problems here, both in the variety of counseling practice and in its interpretation. Techniques involved in communicating the spirit of acceptance may vary, and there are differences of judgment as to the part which explicit interpretation by the counselor to the client ought to play. Ordinarily the psychiatrist does not communicate his feelings directly to the client, and the pastor does not confess to the person who comes to confess except in quite unusual circumstances. Yet the more we know about counseling, the more clear it becomes that the whole self of the counselor does come into the process in hidden if not in overt ways, and that if he is not thus fully involved, the process of therapy is likely to be blocked. Something important takes place *in the counselor*. In Whitaker and Malone's study, *The Roots of Psychotherapy*, the conclusion is stated that the

most important variable in all forms of therapy is the adequacy of the therapist as a person. This leads to a surprising
comment concerning the significance of unconscious factors:

> The common denominator is the interpersonal relationship,
> an interpersonal relationship frequently subjective in character.
> The relationship of the unconscious of the therapist to the un-
> conscious of the patient underlies any therapy.[8]

There are even some theories of psychological healing which
hold that the psychiatrist takes the patient's disease into
himself. The classic case reported by Robert Lindner in
The Fifty Minute Hour of the psychiatrist who is caught up
in his patient's delusions about the cosmos, suggests the
depths as well as dangers of what is happening. Therapy
depends upon an act of identification which yet preserves
the integrity of the persons.

It follows from this understanding of the counselor that
the value system which he holds is not a matter of indifference in therapy. Max Lerner rightly observes:

> The outlook of the analyst is bound to break through into the
> world of the patient. Every word he uses expresses something
> about his values. That is why the analyst himself and his per-
> sonality form a more important factor in the success or failure
> of the analysis than the theory or school from which he works.[9]

The Christian pastor can see reflected here the nature of
the demand upon him when he considers the meaning of
acceptance. For what works with power is the spirit which is
incarnate in the pastor, and without this all the doctrines
and symbols of faith are likely to be quite ineffective. We
may speak about forgiveness, but from whence comes the
power to forgive and to love? That question arises in all its
sharpness when we offer ourselves as Christ's minister in
the care of souls.

If this interpretation of the search for reality in all per-

sonal relationships is true, then we must take another step,
for the person in search of integrity and purpose in life is
never seeking this only in another person. He is searching
for a reality in life itself. What he wants from the counselor
he wants not from him alone, but from life. Note well that
unless what I find in the love and sustaining power of
another person discloses something about all of life, then I
can never fully entrust myself to this love. Recall Mrs.
Oak's statement about her daughter, "She is my only link
with life," and her word to the counselor, "You are my love."
Here the person has discovered what the philosophers call
the ontological question as a matter of life and death for
the self.

Even those who will say nothing about the metaphysical
dimension of the counselor's role will agree that at least
the counselor represents the community, the wider human
environment. The analysis of transference confirms this.
The transference involves the emotional relationship of the
person to the counselor. It has the possibility of helping to
free the person from his bondage to false realities. But the
transference is a transition stage. It functions in healing just
in the measure that through it the person becomes able to
move beyond the stage in which his positive and negative
feelings are bound up with the counselor and to discover
a new relationship to other persons in the family, the day's
work, and the common life. The counselor's function is to
open the way to that new life without his being able to
specify or control its conditions. If the counselor's acceptance
of the person does not have this direction within it, if it
does not look out upon the possibility of a venture of the
human spirit into a larger world, then it is meaningless.

I have been arguing all along that this larger world is
never just the human community, but is the world of man's
dependence upon God who is his origin and his Lord. Thus,

whether we begin with the meaning of the self-image or with the meaning of acceptance, the religious question concerning that reality which is the context of our lives becomes the existential question, that is, one concerning which we have to make a decision. When we give a Christian interpretation of that decision, and speak of personal faith in God who has revealed himself through a personal life, we go beyond what psychological analysis can require, but we are speaking relevantly to the very search which psychological therapy involves.

V. An Interpretation of Atonement

This analysis of the counseling relationship and the acceptance it involves suggests an interpretation of atonement. I do not mean that a new theory of the atonement can be drawn directly from the therapeutic value of acceptance. But it is worth asking why it is that traditional theories of atonement have always left dissatisfaction in the Christian Church.

One reason for this has been curiously overlooked in much of the discussion. The traditional doctrines of atonement have all been founded upon something less than a fully personal analysis of the meaning of forgiveness. This is surprising, since one would suppose that if God has shed the grace of forgiveness in our hearts in Jesus Christ, the place to look for the clarifying analogy would be to the experience of forgiveness in human relations.

The "ransom" theory certainly does not do this. It makes the whole transaction a conflict between divine and demonic power, with man caught somewhere on the field of battle. It makes the important assertion that God fights for us against sin and death, yet it is hard to see how our personal decisions of faith and our acceptance of forgiveness are involved. I think we must hold this about the ransom theory, in spite of Bishop Aulén's insight into the classic motif, as he calls it, and his sound contention that this theory preserves the truth that God is both the reconciler and the reconciled in the suffering and death of Christ.[10]

Anselm's theory of the satisfaction of the divine honor, which has suffered from being woodenly and inadequately described in many textbook accounts, really acknowledges the personal burden of our guilt before God. Anselm never loses sight of the truth which is so important psychologically as well as metaphysically that guilt requires a penalty and a satisfaction if it is to be lifted. Yet Anselm's statement of what is accomplished by the death of Christ does tend to obscure the personal relationship between God and man and to make the transaction valid because it removes a legal penalty and satisfies a point of honor.

The moral influence theories appear to be closer to the personal experience of love. From Abelard onward they see the atonement as God's action in which he shows his love toward us with persuasive power and calls us to respond. But this view has never seemed to take full account of the need for relieving the burden of guilt, and it relies far too heavily upon the belief that the persuasive power of the divine example is sufficient to meet our need. When we recognize the self-giving love of Christ we accept his judgment against our lovelessness. It is there surely that the problem of atonement lies.

The New Testament meets the problem of our guilt at a point which these theories all tend to miss, the personal experience of forgiveness. We may get new light on the personal realities from our analysis of acceptance. The person who cannot solve his own problem discovers one who will stand by him in spite of his burden of guilt or fear, whatever it may be. The person who is accepted does not earn this. He has no claim upon it. It is offered. It is grace.

It is true that psychiatrists and other professional counselors are paid for their services. The psychological function of this payment has many important aspects, but it is clear that the patient buys the psychiatrist's time, he does not buy his acceptance. That is unpurchasable.

Look again at the New Testament picture of the Christ in the light of our understanding of acceptance. Jesus is not the Christ simply because he exercises imperial power over the demons, or because he suffers the results of others' wrongdoing. He does these things as God's representative, his Son, who identifies himself with the human condition. "I am among you as he that serveth" (Luke 22:27). "Father, forgive them; for they know not what they do" (Luke 23:34). What is affirmed in these words of Jesus underlies Paul's understanding of the Gospel, "God shows his love for us in that while we were yet sinners Christ died for us" (Rom. 5:8). In his account of baptism Paul asserts that we are buried with Christ in his death, and raised with him to newness of life (Rom. 6). This is the language of personal relationship and self-identification. It comes from the discovery that God stands by us, in spite of our estrangement from him, that he remains with us in our need, at cost to himself. This is the heart of the New Testament assertion of redemption, and surely this is directly related to the experience of acceptance. We are given to know that nothing in our brokenness destroys the possibility of being understood by another who cares.

There is a second theme to be drawn out which helps us to get beyond a major difficulty in two of the traditional doctrines. They tend to make the calculus of punishment more fundamental than the creative action of love. Now the experience of acceptance has taught us that what happens depends upon the risk of a new relationship where no one can predict or calculate the result. Genuine acceptance is never a matter of balancing the books of life and requiring so much suffering for so much cowardice. We have seen that this element of judgment is not eliminated, but it is subordinate to the creation of a new possibility of life on new terms. Acceptance is not simply a passive reception of the other. It is a reconstruction of the situation, a breaking open both of our need and of our way to health. From this point of view, the meaning of the atoning work of God never has the calculus of guilt as its principal theme. It is the reconstructive action of God beyond all measure of guilt. To be in Christ is to be a "new creation," as Paul declares (II Cor. 5:17). By his redemptive action God has brought a new people into being, the atonement is for all:

> But ye are a chosen generation, a royal priesthood, an holy nation, a peculiar people; that ye should show forth the praises of him who hath called you out of darkness into his marvelous light; who in time past were not a people, but are now the people of God: who had not obtained mercy, but now have obtained mercy. [I Pet. 2:9-10]

We can interpret the suffering of Christ from this point of view. He suffers indeed as a consequence of the sin of men. Through his suffering we have a sharpened knowledge of our guilt. But his suffering expresses the will of God to stand by the guilty one. The theological tradition which tries to separate the suffering of Jesus' humanity from his divinity simply misses the decisive point about the atonement. The suffering of Jesus is the human expression of God's own suffering for us. It is meaningless, then, to speak of Christ's suffering as an appeasement of God. It is rather the authentic disclosure of God's will to stand by us, his creatures, and offer a new life which we do not deserve. Love does not seek suffering, but it takes necessary suffering into itself and uses it in the very work of reconciliation.

When we speak of Christ's suffering as a disclosure of the spirit of God, we go beyond what any human experience can prove, but we find analogies in experience which become luminous in the life of faith. We see why the New Testament asserts that we cannot know the love of God except as it is first given to us in our brokenness. It is never simply a perfecting of what we actually are, but is a new reality remaking what we are. Yet such love has its reflections in our human experience at the point where men offer loyal understanding and care to one another in the midst of human evil. We are continually being saved by it even when we do not recognize the hand of God in the human hands which support us.

We come, then, to the question: "How is it that faith in God's action in Christ has power to transform us?" The traditional theories of atonement have been less than adequate here. Even the moral influence theory relies far too much on our capacity to respond to the divine persuasion. What is it that not only persuades us, but empowers us to live by faith? Here we look again at the experience of acceptance. We are helped by confession to another when we are relieved of the false pride, the pretenses, the defensive shells which keep us from living our lives in freedom. But more important still, acceptance releases power to transform the self because it gives an assurance of a meaningful life no matter what evil or tragedy we face. It is the knowledge that we will not be let go which sustains our will to live. A counselor who had rather unskillfully tried to help a person through a serious crisis by saying that he was "sure the person would come through all right" was long afterward told, "What I most needed to know was not that I would come through all right, but that you and the others upon whom I depend would love me no matter what happened." The counselor regards this as the most important lesson he has learned about therapy.

It is a lesson which tells something about the power which is released through the forgiveness of God. Forgiveness is the offer to stand by and to love no matter what happens. To be forgiven, to accept the divine acceptance, is always to venture into a new order of life which begins strangely and wonderfully enough just where we discover God bearing with us in our present life of fear and distrust.

One of the books on the atonement which expressed this kind of personal understanding was J. McLeod Campbell's in the nineteenth century. His theory that Christ atoned for sin by making a confession of sin for the whole race of men has been often criticized on the ground that the sinless Christ cannot confess the sin from which he sets men free. But in the light of an understanding of acceptance, we can see that Campbell grasped something about the redemptive power of the Gospel which older theories overlooked. He saw the dynamic significance of Christ's self-identification with man.[11] Christ confesses man's sin, not indeed as one individual arbitrarily substituted for others, but in his affirmation of the solidarity of the human community and his identification with its burden. Campbell saw that this act of confession has power to lead men toward a new communion with God. We should not think of confession as a preliminary condition to a later reconciliation. In the light of the psychology of acceptance, confession is a movement within the total action of reconciliation. There is literally no point at which confession leaves off and the new life begins.

V. The Pastor and Acceptance

Psychological acceptance and the Gospel of forgiveness meet in the work of the Christian pastor. However we interpret the theological question of the relationship of grace and acceptance, both are present realities in pastoral care. They belong together.

Forgiveness, as the Christian understands it, involves all that we mean by psychological acceptance. The pastor should find his capacity to enter into the problems of another sustained and increased by the resources of grace to which in faith he turns. Yet it is quite possible to have ultimate faith in grace and yet to fail at the concrete point of showing the spirit of acceptance to another. This comes partly from the limitations of our faith and love, but also from our inability to recognize what specifically is required of us. The pastor will examine himself in the light of the Gospel and of his experience to see how far he succeeds or fails in the severe test of counseling another. He will not lose sight of the ultimate issues of faith which he would bring before the other, but if he is to open the way to that faith he must practice a loyal, patient, and sacrificial acceptance of persons in their struggles. It is a judgment upon the Church and its ministry if, with our belief in God's grace, we repeat the great symbols and doctrines of atonement but actually practice less of a costing identification with the sufferings of men and women than do those who counsel with them under secular auspices.

The pastor shares with the psychiatrist the status of being one to whom others come for help. Like the psychologist, he has his personal problems, and like him, if he is to do his work he must have some basic health and mental poise. But however other counselors may interpret their relationship to those who seek health, the Christian pastor says the General Confession with all men. He stands in the same ultimate need as all, and with all. This is why, when acceptance is transformed into a witness to God's grace, it unites men in the deepest community of all, that which God has created through his mercy shed upon all men, and upon which they all depend.

The word "acceptance," like a good many others, has become in our technical-minded age a part of the special vocabulary of psychology. But, as in the case of so many of the great words, this one has its roots in the biblical tradition. It is in the New Testament that we learn the full power and spaciousness of "acceptance" in relation to the meaning of the atonement. "Blessed be the God and Father of our Lord Jesus Christ," says the writer to the Ephesians, "who hath blessed us with all spiritual blessings in heavenly places in Christ: . . . Having predestinated us unto the adoption of children by Jesus Christ to himself, according to the good pleasure of his will, to the praise of the glory of his grace, wherein he hath made us *accepted* in the beloved" (Eph. 1:3-6). Thus the translators of the King James version rendered *echaritosen,* "objects of grace."

CHAPTER 5

THE MINISTER'S SELF-KNOWLEDGE

"Physician, heal thyself." Those who undertake the care of souls must attain self-understanding. We have seen how the counselor's inner life is involved in his healing ministry. The pastor can obstruct the work of grace if he does not understand himself or his people. That is why churches, theological schools, and laymen are taking a new look at the preparation of the Christian minister. Have we kept theological study in clear relation to the issues of life? The medical doctor who becomes a psychiatrist must undergo his psychoanalysis. Should there be a comparable requirement for every minister? How should psychological testing and theory come into the course of theological study? Some believe that the theological curriculum, with its heavy emphasis on the traditional disciplines—Bible, Theology, Church History—should be radically revised, and that the methods of teaching should be altered to bring the student more quickly to face the question of his faith's relevance to contemporary life. There is increasing interest in field-work experience, clinical training, and similar methods of providing encounter with living problems in theological study. Our task in this chapter is to see what basic principles are involved in the minister's achievement of self-understanding, and his growth toward maturity.

The word frequently used to describe what we are seeking here is "self-knowledge." It is a good term, combining as it does the Christian concern for the person with the psychological emphasis upon facing the self. Self-knowledge includes but transcends intellectual understanding. It means recognition of one's motives, fears, hopes, and habitual reactions. It requires emotional balance, the capacity to face one's past, confess one's limitations and capacities, and establish one's ultimate loyalties. But in a Christian perspective all this is related to man's knowledge of God. We require a theological clarification of the term "self-knowledge" if we are to have a valid conception of its place in theological education. While we concentrate our attention on the training of the minister, we recognize that the issues we are now considering arise in every Christian life.

I. The Meaning of Self-Knowledge

In a Christian view self-knowledge has three dimensions: it is *theological,* for the self is God's creature; it is *personal,* for each self is a unique center of experience; and it is *vocational,* because every self has something to do in the world which requires his special contribution and personal decision.

St. Augustine can be our best guide to the theological dimension. He once said that he desired to know but two things, the soul and God. Augustine prays:

> O God, who art ever the same, let me know myself, let me know thee. When first I knew thee, thou didst raise me up, that I might see what was there for me to see, though as yet I was not fit to see it.

And again he pleads:

> Remain not in thyself, transcend thyself also; put thyself in Him who made thee.[1]

To be sure, knowledge of the soul's relation to God requires something more than theological concepts. It is a knowledge born in the depths of experience from infancy onward. It is clothed with emotion which both reveals and conceals. But the outcome of' a genuine self-discovery is knowledge of the soul's reality and of God's reality as two poles of one relationship. I *intend* something by my life, and the convictions which explain or interpret that intention are "theological" whatever form I may use to express them.

It follows that in any education which aids the self-knowledge of the future pastor, we need something more than psychological introspection and analysis. We need to find those conditions which lie partially within our control through which the Word of God given in the creation and in Jesus Christ is opened to the growing mind and spirit.

We should resist, then, any definition of self-knowledge which confines it to the psychological structure of the individual or the group. But we must not separate self-knowledge even in this theological dimension from the issues in the emotional and mental life which psychologists examine. The Apostle Paul tells us little of the inward experience which accompanied his conversion and his life in the new faith; but that his life was one of continual inward probing is clear in every passage of his letters. In his study of Paul, C. H. Dodd gives his judgment that Paul's spiritual experience and insight show a definite growth from his conversion onward throughout his life.[2] Certainly Paul reveals an internal struggle:

I know both how to be abased, and I know how to abound: everywhere and in all things I am instructed both to be full and to be hungry, both to abound and to suffer need. [Phil. 4:12]

We are troubled on every side, yet not distressed; we are perplexed, but not in despair; persecuted, but not forsaken; cast down, but not destroyed. [II Cor. 4:8-9]

The term "self-knowledge" would no doubt be quite strange to Paul if taken to mean something confined to his emotional life; but his faith was born and empowered in the depths of personal struggle. "For I delight in the law of God after the inward man; but I see another law in my members, warring against the law of my mind, and bringing me into captivity to the law of sin which is in my members" (Rom. 7:22-23).

To put ourselves, therefore, in the hands of God is not to escape the self but to face it honestly. To theologize about God apart from acknowledgment of our bodily and mental feelings is a denial of the truth of the incarnation. God has said his word to us through the person, Jesus, who knew life in this body and mind as we know it. The crucial point is that knowledge of our inner life is in the end knowledge of its meaning, and that is inseparable from the purposes which the Creator has expressed in his creation.[3]

When we say that self-knowledge is *personal,* we stress the unique aspect of every human life. I prefer the term "personal" to "individual" here because the "individual" has too often in the modern period been understood as an isolated atom without relations or responsibilities.[4] The person is an individual in relation to others; but as a person he is a unique center of experience with his history, perspective, and inward life. Alfred North Whitehead's conception of life as dynamic process can help us to clarify this view of the person. Whitehead describes our experience as a series of "concretions, that is, moments of new decisions, each with its relations to the past and to the social environment, and yet each with a novel addition from within the subjectivity of the person to the way in which experience takes shape for him. Our creative freedom lies just in that unique grasp which we have of each moment, adding our perspective and shaping the present toward a future which to some degree we interpret in our own way. Our margin of freedom is small indeed in the universe and among the massive forces of human history; but it exists, and constitutes our dignity as spiritual beings.[5] Whitehead here has outlined in a metaphysical doctrine what Christian faith has always assumed in its declaration of personal responsibility, the reality of our guilt before God, and the possibility of a new response in faith to the grace of God.

It is true to say that contemporary psychology has helped theology recover the significance of this radical personalism. Psychologists have given us fresh cause to realize that the meaning of all our theological symbols comes to us in relation to the struggle to become mature persons, capable of handling the threats and creative opportunities of life. No one knows what Paul's "thorn in the flesh" was; but that it constituted something in his private experience which gave him cause for spiritual questioning and battle, there can be no doubt. Each person has in himself that which must be faced, understood, and used, and which is his alone. The Christian pastor must know this, not only as a general proposition, but as an aspect of his self-knowledge. Not only what he believes, but his way of believing, the route which he has taken to his personal convictions, is important in what he brings to his ministry.

Now indeed the Church has always laid stress on the piety, self-discipline, and maturity of its ministers. Consider the following injunction to those who are becoming priests. It is from the liturgy for the Ordering of Priests in the *Book of Common Prayer*:

And seeing that ye cannot by any other means compass the doing of so weighty a work, pertaining to the salvation of man,

but with doctrine and exhortation taken out of the Holy Scriptures, and with a life agreeable to the same; consider how
studious ye ought to be in reading and learning the Scriptures,
and in framing the manners both of yourselves, and of them that
specially pertain to you, according to the rule of the same
Scriptures; and for this self-same cause, how ye ought to forsake
and set aside, as much as ye may, all worldly cares and studies.

Here are important concerns: a life agreeable to the high
calling, studiousness in regard to Scripture, appropriate
manners, freedom from distraction. How right these injunc-
tions are! Yet we sense that they leave something out which
is vital for pastoral work. They do not, at least in any explicit way, call for that clarification of motive and search
for integrity of the self which we mean by self-knowledge.
What we are needing here is difficult to express liturgically.
Perhaps someday there will be recognition in appropriate
language in the form for ordination of ministers of the need
for self-understanding and clarification of motives. But the
very difficulty of saying this in correct liturgical language
sharpens its significance. The pastor is undertaking a discipline which reshapes his individual and private history.
He must search the springs of human conduct in himself.
Perhaps he learns in a new sense the meaning of the words,
"For their sakes I sanctify myself," for sanctification means
making whole, and self-knowledge is the difficult road to
becoming whole.

It may be objected that to put such stress upon self-
knowledge produces a morbid introspection. Are we not
forgetting Martin Luther's agony over this issue and his
discovery that the Christian is justified by faith and not by
any works, even the work of psychological self-examination?
But we can avoid falling here into the error of the pietism
which seeks to prove its spiritual worthiness. We need honesty both about our unworthiness and our sense of worth.

Each person needs to gain a knowledge of this one self, "Me," of what he is in order that he may give himself without pretense in the service of God and his neighbor. And this requires that he explore the dynamics of the emotional and psychic life. Even the doctrine of "justification by faith," which should set us free from excessive self-examination, can become an impersonal symbol and function legalistically in a rigid personality.

No one can assess the amount of harm which well-intentioned ministers have done through lack of understanding of their own psychological needs, hostilities, and fears; but on any fair view it is quite considerable. Let us put the same point positively. When the minister has begun to be released from false pretenses, from unacknowledged anxieties, and is learning the joy of entering freely into the comradeship of the search for the meaning of life with another person, the high potentialities for his becoming a channel of grace may be realized. It is not only the precious good of psychological health for its own sake which is the goal here, but the release of constructive and healing power. And let us add one more quite necessary point. Health is a mysterious entity, especially when we seek it for the mind. It is surely far more than adjustment. The constructively healthy personalities have for the most part known radical inner struggle. We are not asking for personalities neatly grooved. We are asking only how the struggles we have may lead to creative understanding rather than to despair.

There is a *vocational* dimension in all self-knowledge. We know ourselves through what we do. The Protestant reformers fought for the view that every Christian has a vocation, a calling from God to respond with love and faith and service in the situation in which he finds himself. Vocation in this sense is a fundamental concept in the Christian life, and it will be well to explore its significance for self-knowledge before noting its special implications for the Christian ministry.

Vocation is always a call to action. God, the creator, acts in his world, and seeks our redemption. God's "being in act" is reflected in man's bearing of his image. We are creatures for whom to live is to act. The meaning of "action" is to be broadly taken here. It may be the internal act of sustaining courage in the face of fear, or that of concentration upon an intellectual problem. It may be the silent act of moral decision or strenuous participation in history-making forces. But it is through taking part in ongoing life, discovering what it is to succeed and to fail, to be right and to be wrong, and being baffled by the question of what is right or wrong, that we come to possess our souls. Above all, it is in response to the call to action that we find our neighbor. We find him as friend, loved one, enemy, or mystery, but we find him largely through what we do. Human work is an essay in self-definition. We know how our particular kind of work, job, or profession tends to become inseparable from our personality.

Our vocation to respond to the will of God in the concrete situation presents us with dilemmas of every kind. There are the dilemmas in the conflict of duties. The Protestant reformers identified "vocation" too simply with acceptance of one's place in the social order. Vocation can involve a protest against circumstance as well as an acceptance of it. It is not given to us to know with certainty in every case what is required of us. Indeed maturity is marked by humility about such judgments. The point is that we know ourselves only as we engage in the labor of life, find our capacities in relation to public tasks and private responsibilities, and in the end make some kind of peace with the prospects and the tragedies which attend our lives. The parent makes difficult decisions concerning his upbringing of his children, and discovers himself in making them. One who longs for private peace finds a public responsibility in business or politics. The pure scientist finds himself making H-bombs. The minister who shares all the anxieties and self-doubts of his people finds that they listen expectantly for him to interpret the Word of God. So is the self entangled within the world's life, and self-knowledge comes through discovering what we have to do.

What this means for the Christian minister is that he must win his self-knowledge as a minister. His vocation must be clarified and he must make terms with what it demands. It is often said that the minister must "learn his role," but that puts the point far too feebly, and indeed wrongly, for the word "role" belongs to the theater, and means a guise and form assumed for a dramatic purpose. Vocation is more than a role; it is a life dedicated, and a responsibility assumed. No one should be playing a role at the point where ultimate things are at stake.

The minister has many tasks: preaching, church administration, liturgical leadership, pastoral care. Indeed one of his problems in attaining self-knowledge is the necessity of coming to terms with so many demands, and the discrepancy between what he conceives as his chief ministry and the preoccupation with "running the church."[6] Two points concerning the vocational aspect of the minister's self-knowledge need special attention.

First, the pastor must work out his definition of what is distinctive in his counseling as pastor. He may see that he possesses no final solution of this delicate problem. He knows that in very many situations the special authority and responsibility of the sacred office are at times best kept in the background. But his vocation is defined by the call of God to speak and hear the word of the judgment and grace which comes from God, the Creator-Redeemer. If this truth about what he is doing remains unclarified either intellectually or emotionally then the unresolved problem will foster an inner conflict and insecurity. He will not know his vocation, and yet he will be pretending to have one. This will not do.

I am inclined to think that the sense of reality about "why I am a minister" develops very slowly. It can hardly be otherwise, for the issues touch the whole of life. Very often original images of what it means to be a minister have to be changed through growing insight and experience. There is the shock of discovering what others, either in the Church or outside it, believe about the minister. There is the silent annoyance at being called "reverend," and the loneliness, about which perhaps we are inclined to romanticize too much, but which still is a real problem. And there do come the crises when in personal need or in the shocks of human history we are given to see with clarity the Form of the Servant asserting its power and are humbled and restored by Him who took it upon Himself.

This leads us to the second requirement. The pastor must be a theologian, and the kind of practical theologian who can keep theological concepts in significant relation to human experience. Man is spirit, and the spirit hungers for God. Man is created for fellowship, and his soul thirsts for the love which sustains, cares, and forgives. The theological skill which is required here is that which can go to the spiritual center of the mass of human feeling and anxiety It is the capacity to hear and interpret the unarticulated longing of the spirit through the ordinary language and the extraordinary language which people use. It is the wisdom to know when one is dealing with problems which require a medical or psychiatric diagnosis and which are beyond the pastor's technical competence. This is not to say that there is any human problem where Christian ministry is irrelevant; but that there is no substitute for the technical knowledge and practice of the physician when that is called for.

The pastor needs clarity in his thinking about the meaning of God for human life. The fear of God and the love of God are powerful determinants of emotion, and just for that reason can be easily confused with other fears and loves. God is never remote from his world and from the relationships of persons; yet he is God the Lord, and not a projection of the father image or an unfulfilled wish.

The minister needs theological clarity about the doctrine of God, so also about the doctrine of sin. When someone comes to the pastor feeling cast off from God, human psychology and theological insight must be so fused and skillfully mediated to the person that his way to God may be opened. Here words easily become substituted for reality. In the Christian view of life there is real guilt, not only guilt feeling, yet real guilt can be judged only in confession and prayer, never by psychological analysis or social standards alone. The pastor's task is to open the way for the person to come to confess his real need for God. That means the pastor must be able to clarify the Christian understanding of man's relationship to God and yet intrude as little as possible when the other person reaches out toward God. We see why the self-knowledge of the pastor is a complicated structure. He must know and use the great symbols and concepts of his faith and yet never take refuge in them as if they had meaning apart from their bearing on what men do and feel. He should be able to detect the dry accents of cant, and to speak the words of grace and hope without apology when they need to be spoken.

How, then, does anyone acquire some measure of this capacity? If we knew the full answer, life in the Church would be much smoother than it is, most probably it would be quite dull, and theological faculties would not be continually revising the curriculum of theological study. But in theological education we must have the best answers thought and experience will yield, so let us turn to the meaning of theological education in this context.

II. SELF-KNOWLEDGE AND THEOLOGICAL STUDY

To examine in any detail the many facets of theological education would take us beyond the purpose and limits of this book. A fuller treatment of the problems will be found in *The Advancement of Theological Education*, the report of the Survey of Theological Education in the United States and Canada published in 1955.[7] We are discussing here the theological foundations of pastoral care, and our concern is with how growth in self-knowledge can be furthered in the course of theological study. Every theological faculty knows that the relation between the curriculum and the student's personal involvement is a subtle matter. No one is proposing a special course in self-knowledge, though experiments in group dynamics may come close to that prescription. What are the principles which can guide us in theological education as we attempt to expound the subject matter which grows out of God's self-revelation in history, and see this as it bears upon every man's quest for the meaning of his existence?

Let us begin with the traditional disciplines. The candidate for the ministry studies Bible, Church History, Theology, Homiletics, Church Administration, Christian Education, Pastoral Theology, and so on. There are some who suspect that the enterprise of providing instruction in all these fields inevitably tends to make theological education an abstract and technical process which may never reach the inner life of the person. It is sometimes proposed, especially in the beginning of the theological course, that there should be a deliberate emphasis on the students' personal quest for faith and truth. He should approach his problems "existentially" rather than give nearly all his energy to the mastery of the academic disciplines.

The crucial point surely lies in how we conceive the study of Bible, Church History, and the other fields. Each represents a subject matter derived from the faith of the Church in its historical expressions. Each presents us with a realm of objective concepts and issues which involve technical, linguistic, and philosophical disciplines. But the meaning of the faith and the tradition is surely just the meaning of human existence. To study the Church's thought about God as if he does not matter is simply not to understand what we are studying.

It is right that we should ask the student to concentrate his attention very largely on the subjects rather than upon himself. No one should be compelled to engage in continual introspection about his faith. That may inhibit personal growth. We do, however, need to interpret all theological studies in such a way that their bearing upon real questions is kept in view. There is a crisis for the student when he asks just where this great structure of faith bears upon his personal existence. One of America's outstanding theologians once confessed in an autobiographical essay that his crisis came after he had been teaching theology for five years. Personal tragedy had caused him to face the question whether what he had been teaching was his conviction rather than something not really believed. In good theological teaching we do not try to produce such a crisis, but we should expect it, and try to provide such a conception of the meaning of theological studies that when it comes, it may lead to a matured faith rather than to a destroyed one. What we must make clear is that the minister comes to self-knowledge not as something added to his basic studies, but within them, for they are the objective and significant areas of the faith which he is to represent and serve.

The relation of tradition to present experience is one of the most important aspects of our problem. It is because of the weight, authority, and distance of the past that many students find their study remote from life. There are those who find it difficult to become interested in traditional creeds, forms, and concepts. There are others who readily lose themselves in the past because it offers a refuge from facing the present. For both groups it may be necessary to clarify that dimension of the self which arises out of the past, and which requires us to become ourselves through appropriating the meaning of the past.

To be a self is to share in a community of selves which has a history. In the Church the past comes to us as the deposit left by the experience of people who lived by faith. That tradition offers a fertile soil of meaning in which the soul can grow. We possess ourselves in part by discovering and possessing that past. C. G. Jung's psychological theory of a collective unconscious stream of psychic life with its archetypal symbols as a dynamic source of each individual experience appears to have highly speculative features; but surely he is pointing to an important aspect of the psychic life. It is noteworthy that Freud makes a similar suggestion when he speculates about the origin of the sense of guilt. Apart from the speculative dimensions of these theories we can recognize the reality of the psychic inheritance. There is a psychological dimension in the power of the "cloud of witnesses" which inspires and strengthens faith. That which is deepest in the self is evoked by its encounter with tradition as the self-expression of the community whose heir the self is.

A clear illustration is afforded by the discovery most of us make that we have inherited our peculiar beliefs and values from a special group. It is a critical point in the theological course when the Baptist, Episcopalian, Methodist, or Quaker discovers that values which he has deemed self-evident have been contributed by a particular tradition and that there are others for whom quite different convictions are just as self-evidently valid. We begin to know who we are when we know what our community has been. So the study of Church History can be regarded as an essay in self-knowledge just as surely as a course in depth psychology. Indeed, Church History may offer a special instance, for perhaps more than most theological subjects it is felt by many to be remote from contemporary concerns. But Church History should be understood as an inquiry into why we now feel and live as we do. One Christian psychologist remarked that he believes the resistance of students to Church History is primarily a resistance to facing themselves. Unconsciously they realize that it means self-discovery.

Let us state the principle, then, that every theological subject can be the occasion for self-knowledge. Experience of theological teachers shows that the answer to the question *which* subject will become the key to a student's personal involvement is quite unpredictable. We tend to learn best where we possess certain skills and can experience some mastery. Not all minds formulate their problems in the same ways. Therefore, in pleading for concern with self-knowledge through the traditional disciplines we are not asking for emphasis upon any particular subject. What is required is a point of view toward theological study which encourages the soul's pilgrimage toward what the Puritans called an "experimental" knowledge of God's grace.

Such a conception of theological study proposes no substitute for the patient mastery of the methods and materials of academic disciplines. God's creation, with all its mystery, is an affair of terrible precision. To discover the demands of technical knowledge is one part of the discovery of what it means to be human.

III. Doubt

The reality of doubt is the continuing countertheme to the search for theological knowledge. The community of faith into which the Christian is initiated bears within its collective memory a struggle against doubt, and a continual controversy over the meaning of the faith. It is a prime requirement of theological education that the nurturing religious communities, both school and Church, shall be wise in the handling of many levels of doubt. There is intellectual doubt, which arises from honest questioning of religious belief. This ranges all the way from skepticism as a philosophical perspective to such critiques of Christian belief as the Marxist doctrine of religion as ideological illusion or Freud's theory of religion as wish fulfillment. There is the perennial issue of the adequacy of the mind to grasp the truth of things. How far does Christian faith permit support from reason and from evidence? This question persists within Christian theology—witness the centuries of discussion about the "proofs of the existence of God." Engagement in these intellectual issues is part of the real task of theological education and a substantial part of its power to enlist the mind's full energies.

In our analysis of self-knowledge we can examine here two further aspects of the problem of doubt: its relation to faith itself, and self-doubt as a psychological problem related to faith.

In the Christian perspective, doubt has its profound significance as the antithesis to faith. Faith is more than intellectual assent. It is personal trust and acceptance of the gracious action of God toward us. Faith therefore is mean-

ingless apart from the story of sin and its consequent estrangement. It is we self-centered human beings, caught in
our pretense and despair, who must discover what faith
means. Doubt, then, has a meaning as radical as faith itself.
It is what faith overcomes. It follows that to interpret the
rejection of Christian faith as caused by selfishness or bad-
ness is a kind of caricature of the truth. Of course our moral
failures keep up from accepting the truth of God, but that is
exactly where the ultimate problem of faith lies. How is it
possible that unbelief can be overcome? He who does not
know and confess unbelief in its radical character cannot
know what faith really is. The believer has no right to
separate himself in moralistic self-righteousness from the
unbeliever, looking down upon him as one inferior in moral
strength. In the Christian sense, believing involves knowing
what real doubt is. No Christian pastor can interpret the
meaning of faith unless he knows what faith is up against,
and that means unless he has known what it is to doubt.

We see here one reason why theological faculties are often
rightly more disturbed by the student who seems to have
no religious problems than by the one who does. Certainly
we do not try to manufacture difficulties for the Christian
life. We do not have to. There are enough questions in life
and theology. But there are those who seem to manage to
move serenely through a theological course without any
profound searching either of the Gospel or of themselves.
It is a fair guess that they rarely make good pastors.

When a congregation understands that the minister proclaims no easy faith, but one that he holds only by grace,
they may realize the power of the Christian faith to take
doubt into itself and see it overcome. Frederick W. Robertson was one of England's great preachers in the nineteenth
century. His sermons conveyed, and still do, a sense of reality
in faith which makes us know that here we are on solid

ground. Surely Robertson's power was directly related to his experience in the early years of his ministry of finding his faith almost completely gone. The lonely struggle was intensified by Robertson's morbid temperament, but it reached the deepest levels of spiritual questioning. For a time his integrity seemed to rest solely on his capacity to hold "it's right to do right." But the way was gradually opened to the reconstruction of his belief, and it is fair to say that the sense of reality which his hearers found in his preaching, and which still comes through in his sermons in spite of an unfamiliar style, was born in his personal struggle with radical doubt.[8]

So far we have spoken of the doubt which lies in every man's estrangement from God. Now we turn to self-doubt. It has many psychological aspects in relation to inferiority feeling, repression, guilt feeling, and self-depreciation as a way of gaining attention. As a psychological phenomenon it is complex and has aspects related to neurosis and psychosis. But we cannot set it wholly apart from the religious problem of faith and doubt because, as we have continually seen, the whole self is involved in the search for faith. In Chapter 1 we stated the theory of the linkage of parts of experience to the whole person, and self-doubt is a case in point. We may be baffled by the world's evil and the evil in ourselves, and find faith in God difficult quite apart from any psychological sense of inadequacy. Yet since to know God is to know ourselves in our true origin and destiny, the feelings and struggles we have about our identity to enter into the search for faith. Self-doubt as well as an exaggerated self-assurance can be symptoms of sin or occasions for it. Craving for attention, perfectionism, fear for ourselves, all reflect spiritual self-centeredness.

The sins of the community are reflected in its members. Status-seeking, snobbery, collective pride, can increase the potential for neurotic behavior. What we see in an anxious human countenance comes from within the soul, but it also reflects the failure of love of the community. By the same token, peace and poise of spirit are rooted in part in some sustaining community. The strong self is a tree with many roots.

Say, then, that theological schools and churches should be communities in which doubt is both acknowledged and overcome. If we know anything surely about the spiritual climate in which a person can prepare to be an adequate Christian pastor, it is to be found in a community where faith is a living reality, and where people are unafraid of honest confession of doubt in any of its dimensions.

IV. IMAGINATION AND SELF-KNOWLEDGE

In theological education thus conceived, the Bible and Christian tradition will be studied so that the spiritual conflict which they depict is recognized as our personal history. Scripture is a deposit of faith, but it is more. It tells how the faith came to doubting, suffering, and believing men.

The significance of the realm of the imagination in theological education has been heightened by the new emphasis in pastoral care. We read the Scripture with greater insight when we are also being taught by the poets, novelists, and painters. In part this is because the artists are the sensitive portrayers of life as it is. They tell us who it is we have to speak to. But they also lead toward a true self-knowledge by putting in sharper focus the issues of our lives. E. M. Forster's story, *The Celestial Omnibus,* brilliantly contrasts the excitement which the great poets, Sir Thomas Browne, Shelley, and Dante, produce in an eager young boy, and the snobbery of one who reads the poets to proclaim his cultural status, but who, being brought near to what they can really show him of the height and depth of life, flees in terror.[9]

We know ourselves and God, not by the literal fact alone, but in symbolic visions in which the meaning of the facts takes shape. A theological teacher who is engaged in interpreting the relation of Christian faith to dramatic literature once remarked that he found life interesting because it continually reminded him of things in literature!

Even when the formal theological curriculum does not provide it, theological students who are genuinely searching for truth will usually be found reading in the literature of protest, revolt, and spiritual conflict of their time. Albert Camus' novel, *The Fall,* is an incisive description of contemporary man in his despair and faithlessness. To discuss this depiction of man's ruthlessness and degradation with a group of theological students is to see how one of the great modern spirits, who is not a professing Christian, can sharpen to a razor edge the meaning of sin and the emptiness which is its consequence. Although Camus seems to stand with the atheism of Ivan Karamazov, who will not believe in God in a world where innocent children suffer, *The Fall* is still unintelligible apart from the structure of the biblical faith from which its title comes, and which constitutes its central theme: man capable of love and refusing it. And the novel contains a moving, not altogether clear, passage about the Christ as the one in whom for a brief moment an authentic humanity has appeared.[10]

Artists see many things, not all of them consistent or true. In particular it is well to remember that the *avant-garde* is not always at the head of the procession. A sensitive French critic has remarked of modern literature that it seems to be able only to "paint a faithful portrait of the passions." But he who would know himself and his fellows cannot neglect the self-expression which represents to us the hidden currents of life and feeling. Man is a smouldering volcano. Gerard Manley Hopkins was a Christian poet who understood the struggle for self-knowledge in the twentieth century:

> O the mind, mind has mountains;
>   cliffs of fall,
> Frightful, sheer, no-man-fathomed. Hold
>   them cheap
> May who ne'er hung there. Nor does long
>   our small
> Durance deal with that steep or deep . . .[11]

And a rare Christian novel like Alan Paton's *Cry, the Beloved Country* can tell the frightful truth of man's inhumanity to man and illuminate the whole with the compassion of the Gospel.[12]

What we are urging is a theological education which by whatever means brings about a continual meeting of the Christian tradition with the significant issues in culture. This is one requirement in an adequate preparation for the pastoral ministry.

V. PRAYER

The community of worship and sacramental life sustains the soul in its quest for self-knowledge and the knowledge of God. Worship does this precisely because it turns attention to God and his acts. It celebrates and renews that relationship to God in which alone is our peace. Any note of superficiality or pretense in worship is a serious defect in the Church or theological school. We learn how to worship through participation in the worshiping community. In the search for self-knowledge there is one aspect of the life of worship which we may single out for attention. That is the place of prayer.

It is well known to theological faculties that students feel a special need for guidance in the private life of devotion and prayer, and that they rarely feel they are given sufficient help in this matter. Prayer may become more difficult when questions about God have become matters of intellectual analysis, and the inevitable season of theological confusion sets in. Personal problems such as self-doubt may create difficulties in the devotional life. One effect of the years of theological study is, in more cases than we might readily admit, a serious upset of the life of prayer, and in some cases very nearly putting it altogether to one side for a time. Yet prayer is the soul's meeting with its real help in God, and it is the pastor's privilege to lead the way to a true prayer life. It is good that prayer should not be too easy. Prayer which is not a pious routine but a true opening of the mind and spirit to God shakes us to the foundations of our being.

One secret of reality in prayer is to keep it close to the search for self-knowledge. True prayer is the central moment in which man sees himself as he really is before his Creator. The deepest levels of private prayer, what the Catholics call interior prayer, involve a ruthless honesty and self-disclosure before Him who knows all hearts. To speak of the life of prayer in the religious community suggests at once pious and decorous habit, full of good intentions. All this is proper. In public worship we do not expose all our private emotions. But the personal prayer life is a different matter. It is the one place in life where there is absolutely no use pretending. Prayer is the barren field on which man stands before God, to examine and to renew his final loyalties and engage in battle with the divine claims. Therefore, the very essence of prayer requires our honest thinking about the meaning of our existence. It is real prayer and not merely self-communion when it is undertaken in reverence, gratitude, and openness before that which is greater than ourselves, whatever words or signs we may use. Real prayer seeks what is actual. We remember the bloody sweat in the Garden of Gethsemane.

There is always a danger of self-centeredness in prayer, but more self-centeredness creeps into prayer through the failure to recognize its power to open life fully before God than through any overemphasis upon self-knowledge. A community of prayer ought to be a community of people who have begun to lose their pretenses and who have no need to conceal either their real faith or the hard road by which it is won.

VI. Psychology in the Theological Curriculum

We have left until now the question of the place which the study of psychology, psychological testing, and clinical training have in theological education. One of the widespread movements in theological education in America today, and indeed around the world, is the new emphasis upon supervised training dealing with the practice of pastoral care and courses which will enable the theological student to understand his psychological problems. I am dealing with the theological foundations of pastoral care, and the question of specific psychological methods must be dealt with by those who are competent in this field. What needs discussion, however, is the theological justification for this new emphasis. This lies chiefly in two considerations:

First, there is the principle which has run throughout our discussion of the "linkage" of the various aspects of human experience to one another. Theology by itself never gives sufficient guidance in dealing with human problems, because those problems involve dimensions of experience which have to be understood psychologically. What the psychologist knows about the child's relation to the mother becomes suddenly illuminating for understanding why a particular person cannot accept the mercy of God. By the same token psy-

chology by itself is never enough, for we are led straight
back to the question of who man is and what his life is all
about. What the sciences and experimental inquiries of
psychology and sociology and the rest tell us about man
belongs in the range of the pastor's concern. He cannot
master every field, but he can know something about where
the major lines of insight into human behavior are to be
found.

The second justification for the emphasis on psychology
reflects the situation in which the Church lives in the twentieth century. Too many of the critical questions of modern
life have been kept in the background of the Church's
teaching as irrelevant or indecorous. Contemporary psychology has established for many within the Church as well as
outside it a new kind of confessional. It has provided a
new language in which the emotional life can be discussed.
And through counseling, and group dynamics, it has explored ways in which people can find self-understanding.
There is, for illustration, the sexual aspect of life which is
rarely acknowledged in the usual forms of Church worship,
and where on the whole the Church has failed to bring the
Gospel to bear with relevance and insight. This aspect of
life can be given a forthright examination in modern psychological terms, and it is clear that the discussion leads straight
to theological issues concerning the meaning of creation, the
relation of body and mind, and the nature of the person.

It is not surprising that many Christian psychologists have
an evangelical sense of mission to bring their new knowledge
and experience to the reformation of the Church. This sometimes becomes a new sectarianism filled with zeal to save.
Such enthusiasm can easily overreach itself. The Church
needs the psychological revolution; but this alone will not
save the Church. Let us acknowledge, however, that there
is in the churches today a probing inquiry by people thirsty

for personal release and meaning, and that the psychological movement has had much to do with encouraging and guiding that movement. The psychologist, Erik Erikson, remarks near the close of his book, *Young Man Luther*, that Luther and Freud each did the dirty work of his generation.[13] Psychology has helped man to know himself where the Church either has not understood or has walked too timidly. No one has all the answers as to the place of psychological understanding in the preparation of the pastor, but that it belongs, there can be no doubt.

VII. THE PASTOR'S PASTOR

The pastor needs a pastor. Wherever there is a need in the Christian life, the Church has generally evolved some structure to meet it. The institution may become petrified or fall into disuse, but it is there. The bishop is supposed to be among other things, a pastor to his pastors. Some bishops regard this as one of their primary obligations. It is true that the pressure of administrative responsibilities in the modern episcopacy has tended to crowd out this function, as indeed it has tended to obscure the spiritual role of the bishop.[14] But there are signs of protest, and a new will to reassert the personal aspects of episcopacy. Similar episcopal functions are found in other church orders. In the free churches which have no bishops, superintendents, conference ministers, and others recognize the need to offer to their brother ministers pastoral concern and care. We are concerned here with the need of the Christian minister to bring his problems to a colleague who can be pastor to him. There are three reasons for this:

There is the need for confession. The head of the Roman Church goes to confession. Protestant churches are rethinking the theology and practice of confession in the light of the role of the pastoral counselor. Whether or not we accept the institution of confession as a sacramental and liturgical form, we know the significance of having our inner being disclosed to a mature and understanding person. This is not a denial of, or substitute for, confession to God, but one human condition for aiding a full confession to God. No one can specify just how or with whom the pastor may find this relationship; but there is wisdom in opening the way to it through a conception of the ministry which allows us to offer this to one another.

The pastor needs a pastor also because he needs the continuing criticism and help which can come from reflecting with other colleagues upon the exercise of his vocation. Too often the minister, whether young or old, escapes the discipline of having his work examined by those who can observe critically and judge constructively. One can say that the Protestant minister usually finds this function adequately fulfilled by his wife, and there is no discounting the significance of this loving and expert criticism. But more than this is needed. It is a cheering experience to sit in a group of pastors who in confidence discuss the problems they have undertaken to deal with, the failures they have made, and listen with good grace to the critical appraisal of their brother ministers. There is a resource for insight and mutual support in such sharing. The greatest obstacle to it is, I believe, a defensiveness and anxiety about exposing our incompetence. We need the grace to submit our ministry to colleagues who can speak critical truth in love.

Finally, the pastor needs a pastor because the forms of ministry are being altered in the new pressures of the twentieth century. We need mutual help in the inquiry for a more adequate church life. Ministers are asking in a radical way what, as ministers, they should be doing. This "troubled ministry" has received some public attention.[15] The concern stems not from self-pity, but from an accurate appraisal of the present task of the Church and the inadequacy of purely traditional forms to meet it. Every function of the ministry—preaching, teaching, pastoral care—must be carried on in a new kind of world, shaped by enormous new technological forces, conditioned in scientific ways of thinking, threatened by vast forces of revolutionary political and moral significance. As the minister tries to walk gently in this world, where "lights are dim and the very stars wander," he may find himself so involved in keeping a complex organization running that his margin of energy for reflecting upon where he is headed is reduced to the danger point.[16] His essential ministry remains the same, to follow the Servant in bringing His truth and healing to men; but how that is to be done cannot be decided by old habits alone. We need one another's understanding and pastoral support in the search for a more adequate expression of our vocation.

The aim of ministry is to serve God and his Church, not to fix attention upon ourselves; but without a genuine self-knowledge we get in our own way and in God's way. We have tried to see self-knowledge as a dimension of the Christian life and of the pastor's preparation. Now we turn our attention to pastoral care in the context of the Church's life.

CHAPTER 6

LIFE IN THE CHURCH AND THE HEALING OF THE HUMAN SPIRIT

So far we have given our attention mainly to pastoral care for individuals. Now we must bring to the center of our analysis the fact that the minister-pastor is responsible leader in the Church, the believing community which works in history, declares its faith, and seeks to practice the way of life which it believes its Lord requires. Some who come to the pastor belong to the Church, either nominally or actively; some once belonged and have left; some have been hurt by their experience in the Church; and some are seeking for the first time to become members of the Body of Christ. But in all pastoral care, the Church is present as the context in which the healing power of grace is to be known. Can the conception of the pastoral task which we have been examining contribute to our understanding of the Church? What light may be thrown upon the nature of the Church through the personal experience of acceptance and forgiveness? When we say in the General Confession, "We have left undone those things which we ought to have done, and have done those things which we ought not to have done, and there is no health in us," and hear the Word of the Gospel,

"There is now no condemnation to those who are in Christ Jesus," we participate in the greatest of all therapies. We shall try to see how this point of view contributes to a valid doctrine of the Church. I do not mean that we should conceive the Church merely as a rescue operation for the neurotic victims of civilization; but rather that we see the Church in a true light when we see it as a community of acceptance, humility, and love, in which personal faith can grow.

We can approach the nature of the Church and the work of healing grace within it by considering the doctrine of the Holy Spirit. Charles Williams called his brilliant history of the Christian Church *The Descent of the Dove,* quite rightly suggesting that it is God's presence and power as Holy Spirit which the Church understands to be the key to its being. The Holy Spirit is often invoked in the healing ministry. I shall set forth an interpretation of the Holy Spirit in which we try to correct three common misunderstandings which have beset the Church's life from the beginning: individualism, perfectionism, and immanentism. First we must consider the meaning of "spirit" as we use it in speaking both of God and of man.

I. SPIRIT IN MAN AND GOD

The word "spirit" links the nature of God and of man. In the Old Testament God is spirit, or he has spirit and manifests himself as spirit. But man is "spirit" too. For the Old Testament this means that man is a living, responsible, personal creature of his Creator. Spirit is not an entity separate from the body as a part of man, but is what we would call the whole person, capable of a responsible relationship to God and to other men.

The spirit of God means God himself in his power and majesty as he manifests himself in his self-disclosure to man.

"The Spirit of the Lord is upon me . . ." is the announcement of the prophetic vision. The spirit of the Lord is seen in his creative acts. In the creation story, it is the spirit which moves upon the face of the deep. Israel is called, and its prophets are inspired by the spirit of God. In the story of the redemption, God promises man a new spirit, as in Ezekiel 36:26-27:

A new heart also will I give you; . . . and I will take away the stony heart out of your flesh, and I will give you an heart of flesh.

And I will put my spirit within you, and cause you to walk in my statutes, and ye shall keep my judgments, and do them.

The prophet Joel anticipates the outpouring of the divine spirit "upon all flesh" in the Day of the Lord (Joel 2:28).

Thus in the biblical view our knowledge of the meaning of spirit is inseparable from our self-knowledge. We are made in the image of God. To say we are spirit is to assert that we come to know the meaning of spirit only as we discover ourselves in our relationship to God. Our life, therefore, is a search for the meaning of spirit, not a simple possession of it, even though we are spiritual beings. Recalling the analysis of the three aspects of the self—actual, ideal, and potential—we may say that spirit is not only what we are but what we are coming to be.

Spirit, then, is one of the categories which are fundamental for our knowledge of God, and yet which we hold as analogies and symbols, for we can never claim full understanding of them even as they apply to our being, nor can we assert that we know their full meaning in God. He is spirit. He is active, loving, creative, personal power. This we affirm and yet acknowledge the brokenness of our language which never permits a simple application of any category in precisely the same way to man and to God. Surely spirit is the best category we have, for in our human experience it describes responsible creative being, and yet it suggests the mystery of that being.

In the New Testament we are still within the fundamental pattern of Old Testament faith. But in the New Testament God's action in Jesus Christ has meant a new revelation of his spirit. The Fourth Gospel records the Lord's promise to send the spirit, the Comforter (John 15:26). In the account of the outpouring of the spirit at Pentecost (Acts 2), and in Paul's description of the new life "in the spirit," the experience of the Holy Spirit is connected with God's redeeming love incarnate in his Son, which has overcome the power of sin and death. Matthew and Luke declare that it is through the Holy Spirit that Mary has become the bearer of the Christ (Matthew 1:20; Luke 1:35).

One can, therefore, make a strong case that in the New Testament knowledge of God as the Holy Spirit is always knowledge after Christ, that is, we know who God is through his Son. This view, of course, underlies the Trinitarian assertion that God is at once Father, Son, and Spirit. In the western church the doctrine that the Spirit proceeds from the Father *and* the Son tends to reinforce the view that the Spirit is known only where the Father and Son are together known, that is, through the revelation in Jesus Christ. Of course the Christians already had in their Old Testament affirmations concerning the work of God's spirit from creation onward and sometimes acknowledged this, as in the Letter to the Hebrews where it is explicitly said that it is the Holy Spirit which has inspired the Psalmist (Heb. 3:7; 10:15).

The Holy Spirit, then, means God as he has disclosed himself to us in Jesus Christ. It is not a semidetached divine being with special and odd functions in the world. It is God himself present in Christ the Lord. As St. Paul repeatedly affirms, life in Christ is life in the Spirit, and it is life in the Church. In Jesus Christ God has created a new people which is the Body of Christ in the world. What has been prepared and anticipated in all history has become actual. There is a new people in history "which in time past were not a people, but are now the people of God: which had not obtained mercy, but now have obtained mercy" (I Pet. 2:10).

There are three implications of this view of the Spirit for a doctrine of the Church. Each can be stated over against one of the exaggerations which have crept into the Church's life, often in connection with a distorted emphasis upon one aspect of the work of the Holy Spirit.

II. The Spirit and the Church

God's redemptive action has created a new kind of relationship between himself and men and between men. The foundation of all ecclesiology is summarized in the Letter to the Ephesians:

. . . remember that you were at that time separated from Christ, alienated from the commonwealth of Israel, and strangers to the convenants of promise, having no hope and without God in the world. But now in Christ Jesus you who once were far off have been brought near in the blood of Christ. For he is our peace, who has made us both one, and has broken down the dividing wall of hostility, by abolishing in his flesh the law of commandments and ordinances, that he might create in himself one new man in place of the two so making peace. [2:12-15]

It is the actuality of a new order of life together which is the Church's essence. God has established a new humanity in history, in the midst of the old humanity. From whatever cult or nation men come, the way is now given for them to be members of one another in a new order. Life in the Church ought to be fully personal life, the only such life possible on

earth, because it is the only one in which man's belonging to
his neighbor is affirmed as truth without restriction. Here
we should be able to discover what spirit is, and to know
ourselves through the Holy Spirit, for in Jesus Christ God's
Spirit and man's response have come together.

It follows that the marks of the Spirit's presence should
be found in the *kind of relationship* which men have to one
another. This is the most important insight which the
doctrine of the Spirit can give to us in understanding what
the Church may do to serve the growth of spiritually mature
persons. Yet just here one of the great misunderstandings
of the Spirit has entered in the tendency to look for its marks
in the individual alone, in his subjectivity, even in his
peculiar and bizarre religious emotions. The other side of
the same error of a false understanding of the individual in
his relation to the community is that which finds the marks
of the Spirit only in collective ecstasies where personal freedom and responsibility are lost. The point that the Spirit
is to be found in the kind of relationship where we are truly
members one of another as free persons is so important
that we should dwell upon its significance for theology and
for the function of the church in ministry to individuals.
A brief reminder of some aspects of the modern history of
the Church is in order.

The Protestant reformers quite necessarily stressed the
indispensability of personal faith for salvation. The church
cannot believe for its members. But while the reformers did
not lose sight of the community, they stressed the work of
the Holy Spirit as the inward testimony which makes it
possible for the individual to discern the Word of God in
Scripture; and this made it possible for the churches in a
more individualistic culture to seek the Spirit's presence
exclusively in individual experience.

Unquestionably, the pietism which both Luther and

Calvin resisted, tended to reinforce an individualistic view of salvation in spite of the fact that pietistic mysticism usually stressed experience of the Holy Spirit in the agape-love which binds the community of the faithful together. But pietism found this experience only in the sect, withdrawn in part from the world with its distinctive marks of separation. There are those within who have the experience, those without who do not. That this quite easily leads to an exaggerated emphasis upon individual experience is clearly demonstrated in the history of Puritanism.

Ecstatic sects have insisted that there are special gifts of the spirit marked by highly emotional reactions and expressions. Here again the tendency is either to stress the individual who has these gifts, as in the perfectionist doctrines, or to lose individuality entirely in a collective ecstasy. Roman Catholicism tends to identify the marks of the spirit's presence with the marks of the authentic church as catholicism understands the Church. St. Bernard exhorts his monks, "Do you not know that to obey is better than sacrifice! Have you not read in the Rule that whatever is done without the approval of your spiritual father must be imputed to vainglory and therefore has no merit?"[1] No chance for the Spirit to get out of bounds here! In all these cases the crucial point is obscured: it is in a new kind of personal *relationship,* defined by what man knows of himself through the action of God in Jesus Christ that the true work and marks of the spirit should be sought.

It is in its witness to this new kind of community, that Christianity brings something distinctive to the task of the healing of the human spirit. The Church offers nurture in a community where the human soul can be unburdened, and find a sustaining, accepting love. The Christian pastor should be the counselor most sensitive to the meaning of the kind of personal relations people have, and above all, to the need for the community to which the person can go to discover his true need.

I think it is not unfair to say that modern psychiatry has given insufficient attention to the question of where such a sustaining community is to be found. Of course, psychiatrists know that it is in the interpersonal relationships that the dynamic factors are to be found. But the interpretation of the healing process by Freud, for example, suggests that once the individual has been released from the effects of the infantile complexes all has been done that can be done. Freud's pessimism about civilization contributed to this narrowing of his perspective. He saw no hope for correcting the destructive aspects of the common life. In contrast, the neo-Freudian Erich Fromm becomes quite unrealistically utopian in his hope for the "sane society" of reasonable men, and he never asks where the individual can find in present history the community which can sustain the spirit which must live in this threatening and imperfect world.[2]

What the Church offers is that community in which man's need is understood and his life is sustained by a hope which is grounded on God. If this be the intention of the Church, let us quickly say that it is also the problem, for the church's self-understanding and its practice are often in conflict. What should be a community of accepting and loyal love extending its life to all, is in part a community divided against itself, sometimes adding to, if not blessing, the existing divisions in society and unable, therefore, to give a convincing witness to the faith by which it lives.

One of the reasons psychiatrists have had so much negativism about religion is surely that they have had to deal with the wreckage left by a petty and self-righteous religiousness. They must indeed wonder about a community which exalts the Holy Spirit and has not learned what forgiveness means. We need not indict the whole church unfairly. Even the most loyal and loving community cannot protect people from what other forces in the culture may do to them; but we are required now to state realistically what it means to believe in the Church and this leads us to our second consideration in the doctrine of the Holy Spirit.

We have said that it is in a new kind of relationship among people to which we are to look for the distinctive mark of the Spirit's presence in the Church. That new relationship is one in which the estrangement of men from God and from one another is acknowledged and is being overcome; but it is critical for our understanding of life in the Church that we see it as a continuing participation in the movement of redemption. That movement is to be remembered and continually re-enacted in symbolic ways and in actuality in the church's life. The Church and its members are not free from sin. They are not infallible. They are not free of the temptation to use the very forms of life in grace to support exploitation and injustice. The Church ought to be the community in which we pray continually for restoration to our rightful minds, and where in the humility of such acknowledgment there is ever-new occasion for the renewal of a sane life together.

Let us put the vital point paradoxically and say that one true mark of the presence of the Holy Spirit in any group is its renunciation of the claim to perfection, and its confession of need for forgiveness. We are together *in Christ* when we are in his Church. That means we have been brought by him into a community where the reality of sin is acknowledged, and where we may learn to love one another because we are grateful for what the love of God has done for us. As Reinhold Niebuhr once said in a sermon on forgiveness: "A whole community is a healed community." We are saying that the genuinely whole community of faithful people knows that it depends upon God's healing power, and also knows that healing is never to be treated as its possession, or as a completed work.

It is even necessary to see that the work of the Holy Spirit may create new divisions among men. Christ asserted a new perspective upon life against others. So we may understand the saying about his bringing not peace but a sword (Matt. 10:34). Men have some of their profoundest disagreements over what their Lord requires of them. Consider the divisions among the Christian churches. The Spirit does not blot out such divisions, though in the Spirit we are required to search for the misunderstanding and the sin which is in them. The Holy Spirit will be found where we learn to live in creative conflict, respecting one another's humanity and faith even where we have profound differences over fundamental issues.

We invert, then, the frequent use of the doctrine of the Holy Spirit to support either an individual or a collective perfectionism. The Spirit convicts us of our imperfections, and demonstrates the power of God to bestow a new life in which imperfection is not removed, but where the great good of love is fulfilled in a new and humble community.

Thirdly, then, the Holy Spirit remains God's Spirit, not ours. It is God's communication of his power and truth which we receive in earthen vessels. Prayer is the deepest communion between God and man, yet Paul reminds us that the Spirit prays with us, with groanings which cannot be uttered (Rom. 8:24). He never says that the Spirit becomes one with our human spirit. That is the false immanentism of those types of spiritualist doctrines in Christianity which endanger the clear understanding of the sovereign power of God's grace. To say that the Holy Spirit is God, not anything man possesses, does not devalue the human spirit which bears the image of its divine origin. There is human creativity, freedom, and worth in the order of God's universe. He has given men the dignity of counting in the scheme of things. The human spirit is quickened and fulfilled through the divine inspiration. But man is not God. Even the Incarnate Lord says, "I do nothing of myself" (John 8:28).

There are marks of the Spirit's presence. We see, however, that they should be sought much more in the signs of humility than in claims to perfect faith and love. There are profound emotional expressions of the awareness of God's salvation. The sects which have stressed the doctrine of the Spirit as a release for ecstatic forms of worship may rightly rebuke a staid and too decorous Christianity in which the springs of religious feeling remain untapped. But there is a sound New Testament principle for judging religious forms. It is the principle of the fruits. Paul recognizes extreme expressions of Christian feeling and ecstasy, but he never allows the immediacies of experience to become final tests of truth. He wants ecstatic speaking interpreted reasonably (I Cor. 14). And the fruit of the Spirit is the real test of its presence: "love, joy, peace, long-suffering, gentleness, goodness, faith" (Gal. 5:22).

The Holy Spirit, then, is present in and to the church as the Spirit of God's Holy Love, bringing his people into a new kind of relationship to one another and to him. Everything in the life and liturgy of the Church has its meaning in this new kind of community. It is the real context of pastoral care, no matter how individual and private may be the problems which persons bring to the pastor. And the reality of this community is an empirical and spiritual fact by which the pastor and his people are supported. There is a reciprocal movement between the pastoral task and the Church. If we find the life of the Church a continual support and fulfillment for what the pastor seeks to do, we also discover that the experience of personal and mutual ministry in the Church deepens our participation in the Church's worship, sacraments, and witness to the world. Let us illustrate this point of view toward which our whole discussion has been moving by looking briefly at the sacraments of the Church, the Christian meeting of death, and the Christian life of active service as expressions of the way which is enclosed in the grace of this kind of community.

III. THE SACRAMENTS

In the Church all the experiences of life are surrounded with sacramental expressions of forgiveness and eternal life. This is true even in the churches which give little or no emphasis to baptism, the Lord's Supper, or the other five sacraments recognized in Catholicism: confirmation, penance, marriage, extreme unction, and, for priests, ordination. Quaker silence, for example, has a sacramental quality. All Christian groups give a general sacramental significance to the acts of Christian worship. Our concern here is to consider the significance of sacramental expression for the nurture of the human spirit. Where the Church is understood as a community of acceptance and reconciliation, the sacramental forms will be discovered to have a meaning and power which for many they have lost. St. Augustine defines a sacrament as the outward and visible sign of an inward and invisible grace; but he does not lose sight of the community of believers as the mediator of grace, nor should we, even though our doctrine of the relation of grace to the visible Church may declare considerably more freedom for the Holy Spirit than is the case in some traditions.

It is true that the sacraments are signs and seals of God's self-expression to us, not of anything which the Church possesses by itself; but we have seen in our study of pastoral care that we receive God's grace as persons living in dynamic interchange with other persons. Our response to grace is made in the context of personal relationships where acceptance and forgiveness are always needed.

Baptism surely is a clear example of this significance of the community. Most churches, not all, have held that it can be administered to infants who have no conscious understanding or faith. But the community of faith is there, represented by parents and by the congregation. It is there potentially even where it is symbolized only in the act of baptism itself, as in some extreme cases of the baptism of infants who are without family or relation to the Church. Baptism proclaims the existence of the community of faith which sustains every soul. The community depends upon the Holy Spirit for its cleansing and fulfillment. Hence the act of baptism with its promise of cleansing and renewal affirms for the community its dependence upon grace.

The central sacrament of the Church is Holy Communion, the Lord's Supper. The meaning and power of this Sacrament is for many Christians realized for the first time when they have passed through the crisis of personal failure and have discovered the accepting and sustaining community. It is important for the Christian minister-pastor to help people see the relation between the Sacramental Communion and this personal experience. This does not mean that our human experience alone makes valid the sacramental act. To say that would be to psychologize its significance falsely. What we are saying is that our experience of discovering love mediated through the human experience of forgiveness and renewal is a condition of our participation in the ultimate mystery of God and his grace. Without that participation the signs and actions of the Christian life can become hollow formalities. There are many Christians for whom the sacramental life of the Church and the Holy Communion would have power beyond anything they can at present imagine if a genuine connection should be established in their understanding between the Sacrament and the mutual ministry which is going on all the time in the life of the Church. The signs of the Body and Blood of the Lord broken and shed for us do indeed point beyond the range of our immediate experience. They bespeak the hidden life of God and of man with God. They tell us of that which, in a sense, we are not yet ready to experience. We participate in them by faith as well as by sight. But what they point to is truly present where there is caring and forgiving love. We commune with God as those whose lives are broken for one another, and we find the beginning of communion with one another through Christ who stands between us, as one of us, and yet as the new man calling us into new life. The words of confession, penitence, and trust in grace become new words when they are spoken out of the experience of acceptance.

What is being declared in the Sacrament of Holy Communion is not, then, something merely momentary and immediate. The great corporate and historical tradition of the people of God is present. To realize this can be a check upon the ever-present tendency to self-centeredness in our search for health of soul. The Holy Communion rightly understood will bring its own corrective of a too narrow vision. Those who have faith in the divine forgiveness are participants in the history of salvation which reaches to the creation of heaven and earth in the beginning, and to the new heavens and the new earth at the end. Josiah Royce's definition of the Church as "a community of memory and of hope" is a valid pillar of all sacramental life.[3]

Hope, then, is one dimension of every Christian sacrament. We should stress the sober but confident realism of the Christian faith against all sentimental illusions or cynical despair. In the Christian view of soul therapy we are released to live a new life; but one in which all the great issues are to be faced on new levels and in which hope is an abiding source of the soul's poise and humility. In his account of the tradition of the Lord's Supper as he had received it, Paul includes the words, "as often as you eat this bread and drink the cup, you proclaim the Lord's death until he comes" (I Cor. 11:26). Here in one pregnant phrase is the concentrated meaning of faith's foundation in Christ's self-giving, and its hope for the continuing presence of the love of God.

To say anything about the sacrament of Holy Communion is to have the problem of the divided church bear directly upon mind and conscience. It is true that so-called "intercommunion" is denied today in many Christian churches to other Christians. We should not be superficial in our estimate of the issues here. We rightly guard our theologies of the Sacrament, for the foundations of the Church are involved. But has our theology of the Sacrament lost sight of the love which the bread and the wine declare? The new perspectives in pastoral care we have been considering do not indeed lead to a new theology of the Sacrament, but they remind us that the bread and wine are signs of God's love given for all his finite, needy, wayward people, and thus they may become a source of renewed determination to find the way to reunion at the Lord's table. The word "intercommunion," like the word "interracial," does not belong in the Church's vocabulary. We are not obliged to find reasons for putting things together which are already One in Him.[4]

As we discuss the sacraments let us recognize that the language of the Church has sacramental character. The considerations we have been urging in connection with the Lord's Supper apply also to the very difficult questions which every pastor meets in considering what words to use in the counseling experience. What shall he do with the great words of the faith such as God, grace, and forgiveness, which he knows may be in certain circumstances blocks to a person's understanding of his problems? We can state two principles. One is that the pastor must know he cannot depend upon one vocabulary alone in getting at the realities of human feelings and experience. He must be prepared at times to avoid "religious" words. He should be on guard against using the great words, with their heavy freight of meaning, at a time when people are either not ready to hear them, or are only too ready to seize upon them because they offer temporary refuge from facing reality.

Once this first principle is recognized, however, we can affirm the second, that the pastor's greatest resource, humanly speaking, is the language of the Scripture and the Church, precisely because this is the language of honest confession, of acceptance, and of hope. Speech has sacramental power. The skillful pastor comes to know when the words of grace and hope can be spoken and truly heard, but he knows that there must be preparation and continued renewal if the language is to have its true function. We could say that one goal of pastoral care is to restore to people who have lost it the use of the biblical language and the Church's sacraments. Unless there is integrity in our Christian speech and our participation in the liturgy, the Church is not witnessing as the people of God.

IV. DEATH AND THE COMMUNION OF SAINTS

Ministry to the dying and liturgies for the dead are among the expected services of the Christian minister. The Christian belief in eternal life puts human existence in a perspective which transcends the secular view. Psychologists deal continually with the fear of death and the lure of death, but it is quite clear that many modern psychologists have not known what to do with the meaning of death. Erich Fromm says bluntly:

All knowledge about death does not alter the fact that death is not a meaningful part of life and that there is nothing for us to do but to accept the fact of death; hence as far as our life is concerned, defeat.[5]

Freud came upon the "death instinct," which helped to explain the attraction of danger, as well as some of the internal dynamics of repression and self-inflicted pain. Civilization, he held, uses the death instinct as a means of enforcing the painful demands of work in spite of the ego's basic desire for fulfillment in "pleasure."[6] But Freud gave no clue other than this as to how the fact of man's dying can be taken into a philosophy of life. I have already mentioned the proposal of the Freudian, Herbert Marcuse, for a pan-erotic philosophy of life in which *eros, agape,* and *thanatos* (death) will all be integrated in the one self-expression of the human spirit. But this, he recognizes, remains a hope and speculation. The way to it is by no means clear.

What Christianity asks us to see is that death must be met by faith. Since time "like an ever-rolling stream bears all our goods away," what is the worth of human efforts? Does anything count finally? A philosophy of life which has not asked these questions remains trivial.

The Christian pastor has the ultimate resource of his faith which declares the participation of every life in the eternal purposes of God. Death can never destroy the meaning of life. At the same time he has to learn, in part from the psychologists, that the way in which people react to death reflects all the emotional patterns in the self. There are those for whom the fear of death is the constant over-tone of life. There are others who want to die, perhaps to escape intolerable suffering, perhaps to relieve others of care. Sometimes it is to take revenge upon others. There are those for whom death is regarded as a natural experience and accepted without either regret or support from any religious belief; and others for whom death is a door opened upon a new adventure of life with God. This very diversity of response supports the view that for every person the way in which he understands death reflects in part his unique biography.

This fact that death's meaning is always related and interpreted in experience throws light on one of the difficult themes of the New Testament, the connection of death with sin. The idea that "the wages of sin is death" and that death is in the world because of the fall of man is one theme in the structure of salvation history in the Scripture (Rom. 5:12 ff.). Yet it is difficult to combine this idea with the view that God has created a good world of finite beings, and that death is one natural mark of that finitude.

We come nearer the central New Testament truth in the affirmation that "the sting of death is sin," as Paul says (1 Cor. 15:56). This we can recognize in our experience. As sinners and as men of faith, we find death taking its varied guises. Indeed, so long as we are human, both dimensions are in our experience. Death is known as a threat because we do not have trust and love which God intends for his creatures. When we meet death with anxiety, or with a sense of meaninglessness, we reveal our way of life, not only our concept of dying. It follows that the pastoral task is to help us to recognize what our attitudes toward death mean. Neurotic traits can lead to a preoccupation with death, just as the inability to think about it may betray repressed fears or hostilities. A well-known American journalist had an inflexible rule that the word "death" could never be spoken in his presence. One wonders if this gave him freedom from thinking about it. Keeping in mind the principle of linkage, we see how anxiety about death may be bound up with unresolved questions about the meaning of life.

The Christian faith meets death with the affirmation that

God overcomes this threat to the fulfillment of his purpose by a new action in which he brings all life to judgment and fulfillment in his Kingdom. The biblical expression for this action is the resurrection of the body, thus preserving the doctrine of the unity of man, and rejecting the conception of the soul as a spiritual entity in man which is naturally endowed with the capacity to persist beyond death. This human life, in all its good and evil, its failures, its worth, and its hope, has its destiny in what God prepares for us, not in anything we possess in ourselves. "Whether we live or die, we are the Lord's" (Rom. 14:8), and since the Lord has made his mercy and grace known in Jesus Christ, those who believe in his love know that nothing in life or death can separate them from him.

The connection of Christ's resurrection with our hope of eternal life is understood when we see that it is Jesus, the man who gave his life trusting the divine love, whom we know as the risen and present Christ. It is his disclosure of God's love, standing by man through all tragedy and despair, to which we give our witness in the faith that death cannot hold or destroy what Jesus was and what he brought into human existence.

It is true that modern culture both in its religious and nonreligious moods has tended either to ignore or to sentimentalize this faith in eternal life. Certainly we are not required to think of the new life with God as an indefinite extension of this creaturely existence. It is our participation in the ongoing life of God in whatever way he will open to us. It means that what counts in any human life is not lost or wasted or rejected, but has its decisive judgment and fulfillment in the one history of creation and redemption.

It is necessary to emphasize that in the Christian faith the affirmation of eternal life includes acknowledgment of the divine judgment. Søren Kierkegaard never wearied of declaring, "Immortality means judgment," for it is the meeting of man with God. Therefore, the traditional doctrines of heaven and hell as descriptive of the final state are always relevant for faith. It must be admitted that when Christianity has dwelt upon the promise of heaven and the threat of hell, it has often combined a selfish hedonism with a morbid sadism. Nicolas Berdyaev has remarked that the traditional hell is a place invented by good people to put the bad people in.[7] We can be grateful to modern psychology for exposing the pathology of this sadomasochistic structure as a warning to all religion.

What can be asserted as true in these symbols, however, is that heaven and hell function as signs of ultimate spiritual realities and that they reflect important psychological elements in the meeting of death. The trouble with many conventional pictures of heaven is that they describe eternal life as a vapid and self-centered perpetual enjoyment rather than, as in Dante's *Divine Comedy,* a rejoicing in the vision of God. And the trouble with the traditional pictures of hell is not that they recall the wrath of God and the reality of a final judgment, but that they forget the ingredient of mercy in all God's judgment, and allow the human wish for revenge to dictate the divine policy toward sinners. Christian faith brings realism about death. We can accept both judgment and fulfillment in Holy Love as the reality in which our life is founded. It is this life in its brokenness and need which we offer to God when we leave this flesh. Faith in eternal life is an acknowledgment of our utter dependence upon God, not a demand that he satisfy all our private desires.

When the pastor speaks of faith in eternal life, he will try to show that this faith is a declaration about present reality, not only a promise of something beyond death. The

quality of eternity is present in the love which trusts God
and his goodness. As the pastor speaks to those for whom
death is a problem or threat, the quality of his faith, his
honesty with himself, his acceptance of the limitations of
our human understanding, will be significant elements in
his bringing strength to others. Kurt Eissler has suggested
that in a true communication with the dying, one who loves
will experience death with the one who dies. This is surely
an insight into the ministry of love, and reflects in a humble
and particular way the truth that the Son of God tasted
death for us all.[8]

When we say that a goal of pastoral care is to lead toward
the true valuation of each moment of time as having its
destiny in eternity, we imply no rejection of the worth of
this created world. It is only that we see the greater glory
of the world when we believe that God gives to all times
and places a share in an enduring Kingdom. To experience
this sharing in eternity with other persons is to enter a relationship for which the Christian Church has a special
name, the communion of saints.

We have come, then, to the communion of saints as the
ultimate personal context of pastoral care. It is this community which surrounds each personal pilgrimage with an
inexhaustible source of strength for faith if we will but
accept it. The communion of saints is the company of all
those, living and dead, who have trusted in the love of God
as their experience and faith have given them light. It is
not a perfectionist clique, but the human company trans-
figured. It is not a company of people preoccupied with their
own salvation, but those who through grace have found
their lives by losing them. The great Christian creeds conclude by putting these major affirmations together: "I believe in the communion of saints, the forgiveness of sins,

the resurrection of the body, and the life everlasting." These words do not merely add diverse things to one another; they are related aspects of the constitution of the personal fellowship in which Christ enables us to live.[9] No Christian proclaims his membership in the communion of saints. God keeps that roll with its secrets. But the Christian accepts the reality of that communion as the substance of the new life he has begun to know and upon which he depends. Believing in the community of eternal blessedness, he is bound in love to his neighbor no matter what may separate us in this earthly existence. We die belonging to one another and to Him who makes all things new.

V. SERVICE

We can easily fall into the habit of thinking of pastoral care only as a rescue operation, holding life together when it threatens to become unraveled, or picking up the pieces after the damage has been done. All honest living has these aspects, and pastoral care certainly does. Christianity sees every soul as in need of healing. But the goal in Christian terms is strength to live usefully in the world. Humanity's needs are staggering; it is our responsibility to find our place in doing what needs to be done. Surely there is no greater human therapy than this: to become part of a working group of people who are doing something important not for themselves but for human life everywhere. To find that one's life has use in spite of inadequacies, to belong to a group which will not let us turn our attention always to ourselves but which enlists our concern in the tasks of the common life, is to enter a truly healthy environment. It is what the Christian Church ought to be. The spirit of the congregation is as much a concern of pastoral care as are the special problems of individuals.

It is such a conception of the minister as the leader and guide of a responsible community of Christians at work which gave rise to H. Richard Niebuhr's suggestion in his book, *The Purpose of the Church and Its Ministry,* that the conception of the minister as "pastoral director" is emerging as an authentic expression of the minister's function and task in the church of the twentieth century.[10]

The response of many to the term "pastoral director" is a measure of the inroads which secular culture has made upon the very language of the Church, for some said that to call the minister "director" was to capitulate to the conception of the Church as a business and the minister as its administrator. But through the centuries of church history "spiritual director" has been the Church's name for those who care for souls. To call the minister "director" is only to reinforce that high calling and function. The pastoral director is indeed responsible in the modern church for a highly complex organization. And he may have much to learn from the experience of corporations about honesty and efficiency in human relations. The church has no monopoly on these. But as *pastoral* director he is to give guidance, encouragement, and leadership to a congregation of people who do the work of the Church, and who are seeking to live as committed Christians. The minister does not do it all himself, inside or outside the Church. He is concerned with opening the way for the more adequate Christian service and witness of all, and with keeping all church activity under the judgment of the Gospel.

We learn many things when we see pastoral care in this way. There are those for whom activity is a kind of busy work useful in protecting one from facing himself. All good causes suffer from fanatical and hostility-ridden people who need an inward orientation before they can really begin doing works of love. There are also the "well-adjusted" folk in comfortable circumstances who have not even begun to learn the meaning of Christian love in racial and other group relations. There are the conflicts of conscience in the ethical decisions which work, politics, and all of life press upon us. All of this will be in the mind of the minister as he deals with individuals, and as he seeks to help his congregation realize its true life.

What can guide the pastoral task at all points is the principle that in the mature Christian life personal growth and social action belong together in the integrity of the person. Social action here includes the usual meaning of sharing in movements toward social alleviation or reconstruction, and the wider sense of any deliberate effort to bring Christian faith to bear on the way we live together. It is toward the maturity of life given in concrete service that the pastor seeks to help people to grow.

It follows that one of the greatest pastoral responsibilities is the encouragement of the strong to use their strengths more effectively. To uncover people's talents and wisdom is as important a part of the pastoral task as is care for those in special distress. It might be quite convincingly argued that more insight and skill are demanded in giving counsel and leadership to the mature Christian than to the immature. In every congregation there will be some who need to be carried on the shoulders of others. All need it part of the time. And there are always those who prefer the sickness to the cure in matters of spirit as well as of body. But there are others who by grace do become centers of strength in their faith, their insight, and their courage. The pastor is concerned with all as he seeks to enlist each in the service of God. It is for him and his people to learn and relearn that our life has its meaning in accepting the Form of the Servant, no matter what the measure of our present power to do so may be.

VI. THE SPIRIT IN THE CHURCH

All the lines of thought we have been exploring lead to one conclusion about the Church: It is the true Christian community holding out hope for the nurture and health of spirit of those within it when it is animated by the spirit of acceptance, of reconciliation, and of service. In the Church we always live beyond our spiritual depth. The vision and hope of the Christian faith lend to each one a stature he does not merit of himself. The Church truly lives by hope. But the foundation of that hope is something which can be claimed without sentimentality or pretense. That is the experience of learning and practicing a genuine acceptance of one another and a sacrificial caring for one another. Such love can inform the spirit of a congregation, and be the power of saving grace for those whom it touches. In his ministry to individuals the pastor must never lose sight of the significance of the kind of community the church is in its basic intention. The spirit of the reconciling community is, to be sure, never created by our giving constant attention to our intimate feelings. It comes mainly through acceptance of the tasks God sets for us to do, and our seeking to be his Church in a difficult world. But in the absence of this spirit in the Church, the mending of broken souls will have to turn to other auspices.

There are problems to be solved to keep the Church such a community. There is the tendency of our religiousness toward "moralism" in the bad sense, that is, toward a rigid and self-righteous judgment according to a moral standard which we assume puts us in a good light and others in a bad. It is easy to condemn moralism; it is much harder to see how the Christian Church can live both as a community of forgiveness and yet as a community with loyalty to a high ideal of conduct. Plain ordinary respectability is a good, and the Church cannot ignore it. But can the congregation put respectability in the second place as our Lord did when it is necessary to the saving of souls? That is a test.

The forms of church life may either help or block the growth of an understanding community. There is good reason to think that some of the important things can happen only in groups small enough to permit deep and personal sharing of experience over a considerable period of time. The growth of such groups of inquiry and sharing is one of the significant movements in the churches at the present time. These groups are not substitutes for the total life of the congregation in worship and witness; but they may be a most important means of breaking through rigidities and opening up a frank discussion where there will be no fear of probing sacred symbols and doctrines.

Our theme has been the care of souls, and we have discussed this theme in relation to the work of the Christian minister-pastor. We have seen, however, that it is neither to the Church nor to the pastor in the first instance that the care of souls belongs. It is God in his supreme act of love in Jesus Christ who heals the human spirit. The pastoral task, as it comes to every minister and every Christian, is to respond to the wonder of God's care for the soul and to share with others such knowledge as he has of God's healing power.

NOTES

Chapter 1, Therapy and Salvation: The Dimensions of Human Need

1. See Johannes Hempel, *Heilung als Symbol und Wirklichkeit im biblischen Schrifttum* (Gottingen, 1958); George Johnston, "Soul Care in the Ministry of Jesus," *Canadian Journal of Theology*, Vol. V and Vol. VI, No. 1 (1959-60); W. A. Jayne, *The Healing Gods of Ancient Civilizations* (New Haven: Yale University Press, 1925).
2. H. Wheeler Robinson, *Redemption and Revelation* (New York: Harper & Brothers, 1942), p. 232.
3. Paul Tillich, *Systematic Theology*, Vol. II (Chicago: University of Chicago Press, 1957), p. 93.
4. J. McLeod Campbell, *The Nature of the Atonement* (Cambridge: Macmillan, 1856), p. 283.
5. In *Paul and Rabbinic Judaism* (London: S.P.C.K., 1955), p. 149, W. D. Davies has shown that Paul regarded Jesus as the new Torah, but he makes clear that the concept of Torah transcended legalistic connotations.
6. William Ernest Hocking, *Human Nature and Its Remaking* (New Haven: Yale University Press, 1929), chap. 3.
7. Augustine, Serm. 123, iv, 4.
8. John Calvin, *Institutes of the Christian Religion*, III, 3. 10.
9. Erik Erikson, *Young Man Luther* (New York: W. W. Norton, 1958), p. 253.
10. Herbert Marcuse, *Eros and Civilization* (Boston: Beacon Press, 1956).
11. Erich Fromm, *Man for Himself* (New York: Rinehart & Co., Inc., 1947), p. 159. The quotation continues: "Humanistic conscience can be justly called the *voice of our loving care for ourselves.*"
12. Henry N. Wieman, *Man's Ultimate Commitment* (Carbondale: Southern Illinois University Press, 1958), chap. 3.
13. Martin Luther, from *Tischreden*, I, p. 352 (Weimar, ed.), quoted in Erikson, *op. cit.*, p. 251.

Chapter 2. The Minister's Authority

1. T. W. Manson, *The Church's Ministry* (Philadelphia: Westminster Press, 1948), p. 30.
2. John T. McNeill, *A History of the Cure of Souls* (New York: Harper & Brothers, 1951).

H. R. Niebuhr and Daniel D. Williams (eds.), *The Ministry in Historical Perspectives* (New York: Harper & Brothers, 1956).

3. John Oman, *Grace and Personality,* 3rd ed. rev. (Cambridge: The University Press, 1925), p. 225.

4. Erich Fromm, *The Sane Society* (New York: Rinehart & Co., Inc., 1955), p. 351.

5. N. Berdyaev, *Slavery and Freedom* (New York: Charles Scribner's Sons), Pt. IV, 1.

6. Donald Baillie, *God Was in Christ* (New York: Charles Scribner's Sons, 1948), p. 127.

7. From an unpublished monthly report to the Administrative Board of the East Harlem Protestant Parish, no date (about 1958).

8. Cf. Carroll A. Wise, *Religion in Illness and Health* (New York: Harper & Brothers, 1942), pp. 222-23.

CHAPTER 3.   PERSONAL CHANNELS OF GRACE

1. Recent developments of existentialist theories in psychotherapy are a case in point. See Rollo May *et al., Existence* (New York: Basic Books, 1958); and H. Mullah and I. A. Sangiuliano, "Interpretation as Existence in Analysis," in *Psychoanalysis and Psychoanalytic Review,* Vol. 45, Nos. 1-2 (1958).

2. Cf. Seward Hiltner, *Pastoral Counselling* (New York: and Nashville: Abingdon Press, 1949).

3. C. G. Jung, *Psychology and Religion* (New Haven: Yale University Press, 1938), p. 114.

4. C. G. Jung, *Answer to Job* (London: Routledge and Kegan Paul), 1954.

5. Professor Paul Ricoeur of the Sorbonne took this view in a seminar at Columbia University in 1958.

6. Carl R. Rogers, "The Case of Mrs. Oak: A Research Analysis," in *Psychotherapy and Personality Change,* edited by Carl R. Rogers and Rosalind F. Dymond (Chicago: University of Chicago Press, 1954).

7. *Ibid.,* p. 268.

8. *Ibid.,* p. 324.

9. *Ibid.,* p. 333.

10. *Ibid.,* p. 337.

11. *Ibid.,* p. 342. (The numbering of these selected paragraphs is my own.)

12. S. Freud, *A General Introduction to Psychoanalysis,* Eng. trans. (New York: Liveright, 1935), p. 387. (Perma Books ed., p. 453.)

13. *Ibid.,* p. 387.

14. *The Case of Mrs. Oak,* p. 311.

15. William Ernest Hocking, *Science and the Idea of God* (Chapel Hill: University of North Carolina Press, 1944), p. 41.

16. Rollo May in a public lecture given at Union Theological Seminary, New York, April 6, 1959.

17. Paul Tillich, *Systematic Theology*, Vol. I (Chicago: University of Chicago Press, 1951), p. 288.

18. Somerset Maugham, *The Summing Up* (New York: New American Library edition, 1946), p. 36.

19. Cf. H. Wheeler Robinson, *Redemption and Revelation* (New York: Harper & Brothers, 1942), p. 271.

CHAPTER 4. FORGIVENESS, JUDGMENT, ACCEPTANCE

1. Gene Fowler, *Good Night, Sweet Prince,* (New York: Viking Press, 1944), p. 136.

2. C. G. Jung, *The Integration of the Personality* (New York: Farrar & Rinehart, 1939).
   S. Freud, *A General Introduction to Psychoanalysis*, Lecture XXI.

3. Paul Tillich, "Heal the sick, cast out demons," *Union Seminary Quarterly Review*, Vol. XI, No. 1 (1955).

4. Karen Horney, *Neurosis and Human Growth* (New York: W. W. Norton & Co., Inc., 1950), p. 158.

5. William Ernest Hocking, *The Self: Its Body and Freedom* (New Haven: Yale University Press, 1928), p. ix.

6. William J. Wolf, *No Cross, No Crown* (New York: Doubleday & Company, 1957), pp. 149 ff.

7. Paul Tillich, *The Courage to Be* (New Haven: Yale University Press, 1952), pp. 167 ff.

8. C. A. Whitaker and T. P. Malone, *The Roots of Psychotherapy* (New York: Blakistan, 1953), p. 65. I am indebted to Charles Stinnette for directing me to this statement.

9. Max Lerner, "Is Analysis Dangerous?" *New York Post*, Feb. 13, 1958.

10. Gustav Aulén, *Christus Victor* (New York: Macmillan Co., 1931).

11. J. McLeod Campbell, *The Nature of the Atonement* (Cambridge: Macmillan, 1856), *passim*.

CHAPTER 5. THE MINISTER'S SELF-KNOWLEDGE

1. Augustine, *Confessions*, VII, x, 16.

2. C. H. Dodd, "The Mind of Paul: I," in *New Testament Studies* (New York: Charles Scribner's Sons, 1952), pp. 77-82.

3. John Calvin, *Institutes of the Christian Religion*, I, 1.

4. Cf. Jacques Maritain, *Christianity and Democracy* (New York: Charles Scribner's Sons, 1944), pp. 57 ff.

5. Alfred North Whitehead, *Process and Reality* (New York: The Macmillan Company, 1936), Pt. II, Sec. I, Sec. 4; Pt. III, chap. 1-3.

6. Samuel Blizzard, "The Parish Minister's Self-Image and Variability

in Community Culture," *Pastoral Psychology*, Oct., 1959; "The Minister's Dilemma," *The Christian Century*, Vol. 73, April 25, 1956.

7. H. Richard Niebuhr, Daniel D. Williams, and James M. Gustafson (New York: Harper & Brothers, 1955).

8. *The Life and Letters of Frederick W. Robertson*, edited by Stafford H. Brooke (Boston, 1865), Vol. I.

9. E. M. Forster, *The Celestial Omnibus and Other Stories* (New York: A. A. Knopf, 1923).

10. Albert Camus, *The Fall*, English trans. (New York: Alfred A. Knopf, 1957).

11. Gerard Manley Hopkins, Sonnet "41."

12. Alan Paton, *Cry, the Beloved Country* (New York: Charles Scribner's Sons, 1948).

13. Erik Erikson, *Young Man Luther* (New York: W. W. Norton, 1958), p. 9.

14. Cf. K. E. Kirk, *The Apostolic Ministry* (New York: Morehouse-Gorham, 1946).

15. Cf. Wesley Shrader, "Why Ministers Are Breaking Down," in *Life*, Aug. 20, 1956; comments by Roy Pearson and Daniel D. Williams in *Christianity and Crisis*, Vol. XVI, Nos. 18, 21.

16. The line is from Gilbert Murray. I am indebted to Wayne Oates for it.

CHAPTER 6. LIFE IN THE CHURCH AND THE HEALING OF THE HUMAN SPIRIT

1. Bernard of Clairvaux, *On the Song of Songs*, Sermons 13, 15, 18-20. In edition by a religious of C.S.M.V. (London: A. R. Mowbray & Co., 1952), p. 49.

2. S. Freud, *Civilization and Its Discontents* (New York: J. Cape & H. Smith, 1930).

Erich Fromm, *The Sane Society* (New York: Rinehart & Co., Inc., 1955).

It is curious that in spite of the great optimism with which Fromm writes about man, he says in this book, "It is man's fate that his existence is beset by contradictions, which he has to solve without ever solving them" (p. 362).

3. Josiah Royce, *The Problem of Christianity* (New York: The Macmillan Company, 1914), Vol. II, p. 72.

4. The ecumenical problem of the Church is directly related to the problem of pastoral care. I have written elsewhere a proposal concerning unity at the Lord's table. "Intercommunion at Lund," *The Ecumenical Review*, Vol. V., No. 4, (1952-3)

5. Erich Fromm, *Man for Himself* (New York: Rinehart & Co., Inc., 1947), p. 42.

6. S. Freud, *Civilization and Its Discontents* (Westport, Conn.: Associated Booksellers), p. 74.

7. N. Berdyaev, *The Destiny of Man* (New York: Charles Scribner's Sons, 1937), pp. 345-46.

8. Kurt Eissler, *The Psychiatrist and the Dying Patient* (New York: International University Press, 1955).

9. I am indebted to Robert McAfee Brown for an important suggestion about the interrelatedness of the creedal affirmations.

10. H. Richard Niebuhr, *The Purpose of the Church and Its Ministry* (New York: Harper & Brothers, 1956), pp. 79 ff.

Gentlemen:

About a year ago we sold a home in which we had resided for about 5 years, and which subsequently we rented upon our transfer only 9 from the area.

To our shock we recently learned of only days ago a "capital gains" underledwe in an amount to IRS which we simply are not in a position to pay. The proceeds of the sale have been reinvested in our new in the purchase of our new home; in the belief that we believed that were such reinvestment of our equity further 18 months we could protect done we had or in which to do so. our "gain".

I have taken a new job which is a straight commission from which to date I've not earned $1.00. My wife take home $800.00, a bit more than enough to pay our mos monthly home payments.

Our appeal is for an extension of several after which we will months to "get our act together". Thank you. Yours to had

Need an installment arrangement spread out o a year or so if we're to pay all our obligate

INDEX

As a person with strong objections to the use of ~~moon~~ tax monies by the gov't ~~for~~ to support the military-industrial Mason, I have long felt my helplessness.

Example: Foreign aid sends expensive military hardware to both sides of a conflict i.e. Israel: Egypt as an enormous cost to the taxpayer. Not to speak of the folly of putting a gun in the hands of two enemies — an excellent way to inspire war — but a ~~an~~ dubious political technique at best. The U.S. can't please both sides.

I am also a clergyman & a Christian — Because % of said budget goes for military purpose in one form or another, for reasons of conscience I've elected to deduct that amt from our income & prop. tax for yr. 1978⁻ and hope that my constitutional right of dissent will be respected by ~~the~~ ~~Int'l~~ I.R.S. — an organization which is becoming increasingly suspect in the area of human rights.

~~Thank You~~   WDD

Ch 3 is segregated fn → Lecture I —

137-138   At basic our   56 61 M — lectures — on
          of all many question is religious —   meaning
              who we may not attend f then that 64 # — nature of univ
          self, nature etc   96 Know yourself — 9.
                                                  Augustine etc
12-3 Man — as spirit

1/4 oort Hell — a place nourished by God
140   people to put God first w —

103 on roles

Cross Series 6 g - 9

W phone Mr Kogerinis —
his home should now go in
escrow.